More Praise for HOW *SASSY* CHANGED MY LIFE

"Around the time you read that a publicist for Tiffani Amber-Thiessen once accused *Sassy* magazine of 'terrorist tactics,' you realize that this book isn't simply a smart and funny ode to a smart and funny magazine; it's the record of a short-lived insurrection against a powerful social code, one that tells young women what they're supposed to think and how they're supposed to act."

—ALEX ROSS, music critic of *The New Yorker*

"*Sassy* really did change my life. If I hadn't read the magazine as a confused preteen, I doubt I'd be the person I am today and I doubt I'd have started *Venus Zine*. I always wanted to know what really happened behind the scenes at *Sassy*, and this book provides the inside scoop on its rise and fall."

—AMY SCHROEDER, editor and publisher of *Venus Zine*

"It is perhaps a sad fact that magazines come and go. But in its brief life, *Sassy* offered teenage girls a new way of seeing themselves—and their parents, perhaps, a new way of understanding them. The publication was very much a product of its historical moment. Furthermore, as this insightful narrative suggests, *Sassy*, like all truly significant magazines, clearly helped shape the social realities of its time."

—DAVID ABRAHAMSON, Charles Deering McCormick Professor of Teaching Excellence, Medill School of Journalism, Northwestern University

"An entertaining and thought-provoking look at one of the most influential magazines of the nineties. I felt like I was back in those cramped offices, surrounded by the funniest, sharpest women in New York."

—BLAKE NELSON, author of *Girl* and *Paranoid Park*

How
SASSY
Changed
My Life

· · · · ·

SASSY NOVEMBER 1989
SASSY APRIL 1990
sassy jan. 91
SASSY JANUARY 1990
sassy july '93
SASSY MAY 1990
SASSY MARCH 1990
sassy feb. 91
sassy may '92
SASSY APRIL 1990
SASSY SEPTEMBER 1994
SASSY AUGUST 1994
SASSY NOVEMBER 1994
SASSY OCTOBER 1993
SASSY JANUARY 1994
SASSY MARCH 1988
SASSY JULY 1994
SASSY FEBRUARY '93
SASSY DEC. 91
sassy april 1994
SASSY MAY 1994
SASSY JULY 1990
SASSY JUNE 1990
SASSY MAY 1989
SASSY JULY 1989
sassy april '93
sassy december '92
SASSY MAY 1989
SASSY FEBRUARY 1990
sassy sept. 91
sassy feb. 92
sassy october '92
SASSY FEBRUARY 1990
SASSY SEPTEMBER 1989
SASSY NOVEMBER 1988
SASSY JULY 1988
SASSY JUNE 1988
SASSY MAY 1988
SASSY JUNE 1989
sassy september '92
SASSY SEPTEMBER 1988
SASSY APRIL 1989
sassy december '92
SASSY JUNE SEPTEMBER 1988

TOO COOL FOR SCHOOL
CHANGE THE WORLD
GET SET...
not a warner bros. house organ
corporate zine
MAY BE...MAYBE NOT
OFF THE DEEP END
THE WORKS
FOR THE BIRDS
WHAT IS THE MEANING OF LIFE?
LOVE IS A DOG
THE QUESTION IS, WHAT ARE
A SOFT PATINA OF NAUSEA
TOTAL MAYHEM
corporate zine
SCHOOL IS BLOWN TO PIECES
ROBERT + CHRISTINA = 4EVA
NOW WE ARE SIX
IF YOU CAN SMELL IT, IT'S KILLING YOU
nature of a plagiariza
LISTEN UP, SISTAS
WOULD YOU LIKE FRIES WITH THAT?
I DREAMED I WAS ASSERTIVE
ON YOUR MARK...
then again, perhaps not
NATHAN HAS BOY DISEASE
COMPETITION? WHAT COMPETITION?
IF THEY CALL YOU A FAT PIG, SAY THANK YOU
THE FRESHMAKER
DID YA BELT 'EM? DID YA CINCH 'EM?
valentines, schmalentines
wheeeeeeeeeeeeeel!
I WANT TO GO HOME NOW
ALSO: 8 SURFERS, 7 DOGS, 6 CATS, MANY FISH, MRS. CATCHPOLE AND MORE
RECYCLE THIS
r.i.p. tom carvel, 1906—1990
THANKS
"'90210' is rootless!"
For a good time call 1·202·456·1111
"The question is what are you doing?" says MK

How SASSY Changed My Life

a love letter
to the greatest
teen magazine
of all time

· · · · ·

KARA JESELLA and
MARISA MELTZER

faber and faber, inc.

An affiliate of Farrar, Straus and Giroux

New York

Faber and Faber, Inc.
An affiliate of Farrar, Straus and Giroux
19 Union Square West, New York 10003

Library of Congress Cataloging-in-Publication Data
Jesella, Kara, [date]
    How Sassy changed my life : a love letter to the greatest teen magazine of all time /
  by Kara Jesella and Marisa Meltzer. —1st ed.
      p.   cm.
    ISBN-13: 978-0-571-21185-2 (pbk. : alk. paper)
    ISBN-10: 0-571-21185-2 (pbk. : alk. paper)
    1. Teenage girls—United States—Attitudes.   2. Sassy (New York, N.Y. : 1988)—History.
  3. Feminism—United States.   I. Meltzer, Marisa, [date]   II. Title.

  HQ798.J39 2007
  305.235'20973—dc22

                                                            2006030415

Designed by Charlotte Strick

www.fsgbooks.com

10   9   8   7   6   5   4   3   2   1

contents

introduction

"Why would you write a book about a teen magazine?"

We've lost count of how many times we've been asked some version of that question since this project began.

Luckily, the floods of emails we got from people saying they couldn't wait until its publication and asking how they could help served as an excellent emotional buffer from the blank stares. Smart, cool women who grew up reading and loving *Sassy* offered to be interviewed; staff members and interns assured us they would let us know what really went on in the magazine's offices; celebrities who had special relationships with the publication—like Spike Jonze and Michael Stipe—wanted to pay their respects.

Because more than a decade after the publication's untimely and much-lamented demise, *Sassy* matters as much as it did when it was in print. Though *Sassy* was never able to match the advertising or circulation of the other teen magazine giants of its day, the magazine more than made up for this lack in terms of reader devotion.

Even now, it continues to incite cultlike dedication among its fans. Copies on eBay inspire heated bidding wars. ("Fifteen years later, a weird kind of muscle memory takes over when I finally get my vintage *Sassy*," said Rebecca L. Fox in a paper called "*Sassy* All Over Again" for NYU journalism school. "To my surprise, I read *Sassy* now the same way I read it in my teens—voraciously.") Magazines feature sentimental stories mourning it: "We Still Love *Sassy*" was the bittersweet title of an article that ran in *The New York Review of Magazines*. On the Internet, message boards and open love letters to the *Sassy* staff abound: "You gave us thirteen-year-old girls stuck in rural Wisconsin a glimmer of hope, a pinky-swear promise that the world could be a funny, smart, and even sexy place," wrote one Harvard student in the *Crimson*. "I loved *Sassy* so much, and needed it so much, and it was there for me," a Swarthmore student said on her Web site.

A 1997 article in *Spin* magazine's Girl Issue noted: "When the best teen magazine ever, *Sassy*, was sold to the owners of *Teen* magazine in 1994—and the entire New York–based staff was put out to pasture—readers went into revolt. *Teen* magazine exemplified everything that was wrong with America's youth, and *Sassy* was its antithesis. Distraught teenagers tracked down staff members at home, calling with a simple question: Why?"

"Why?" is just one of the questions that this book will answer. *How* Sassy *Changed My Life* is the inside story of how and why the magazine came to be, what happened during its six short years of life, and the real reasons behind its demise. More important, it is a tribute to a monumentally significant cultural artifact that has been given short shrift.

Understanding *Sassy*'s importance begins with a chronicle of the early days of the magazine and how it distinguished itself. *Sassy*'s story is intricately tied to the societal transformations that occurred in the late eighties and early nineties. As teen-pregnancy rates soared, AIDS became a very real threat, and debates over what kids should be taught about sex in school raged, the magazine heralded a new way of thinking about girls and sexuality; we will discuss how this led to a battle with the religious right—then just becoming a force to be reckoned with—that almost put the magazine out of business.

To best explain the scope of *Sassy*'s impact, and the major themes that characterized the magazine's middle years, it's key to bear in mind events that were happening simultaneously. At a time when the cultural mainstream and underground were two distinct entities, *Sassy* relentlessly covered indie celebrities and tenets of indie culture for the masses, while at the same time deconstructing pop tarts. As the victories of Second Wave feminism and the new ideas of the Third Wave crystallized, *Sassy* heralded a changing of the guard in the women's movement and brought a new version of feminism to high-school girls. And while teenagers who obsessed over *90210*, lipstick, and just wanting to have fun had long been denigrated as silly and fluffy, the magazine made being a girl seem vital and important, creating a new kind of female persona—one that very much still exists today. In an era of political and economic flux—first a Republican president, then a Democrat; first a boom time for magazines, then a recession—*Sassy* struggled to maintain a resolutely progressive voice, which by its very nature couldn't last. "Every six or seven years something comes along that's just exactly right," says writer Blake Nelson. "*Sassy* was just exactly right." And its considerable legacy is no surprise. As we'll see, for readers, pining for *Sassy* is about more than revisiting another era.

Certain institutions link people together irrevocably: a fifty-year-old Tri-Delt meets a twenty-five-year-old Tri-Delt and they are instant sisters; *Sassy* serves a similar purpose, but for a different psychographic. Julianne Shepherd thinks she got a former job as arts editor of the *Portland Mercury*, a weekly in Portland, Oregon, because "in the interview, I noted *Sassy* as a major influence on my inchoate writing voice, and the publisher, Tim Keck [who co-founded *The Onion* in 1988 when he was a junior at the University of Wisconsin], was essentially like, 'Right on! You're hired!' "

In other words, *Sassy* has become a kind of code. "I meet people now and occasionally ask them if they were *Sassy* readers," says fan Catherine Bowers. Upon meeting a fellow *Sassy* fan, we feel like we understand something essential about that person: their life philosophy, what their politics might be like, what their artistic preferences are, what they were like in high school, what kind of person they wanted to grow up to be. (By contrast, we find non-fans of a certain age slightly suspect.) We seem to recognize kindred spirits even now. "A lot of us *Sassy*-ites found each other," says fan Lara Zeises. None of her friends

read it in high school, she says, "but most of my friends now were of the *Sassy* generation, and it's like we have this special bond because of it."

It's faith in that "special bond" that enabled us to decide to write a book about *Sassy* together about half an hour—tops—after we met.

To explain: "I really think *Sassy* changed my life," said Marisa, over drinks. We were discussing a story she was going to write for the teen magazine Kara worked for at the time.

"I know!" Kara agreed. "I don't understand why no one has ever written a book about it."

We talked about how much we would love it if there was a *Sassy* tribute book, something that would tell *Sassy*'s unusual story and explore the ways in which it affected thousands of girls like us—not to mention its legions of non-girl fans.

"We should write it," said Marisa. We started immediately. Although we didn't know anything more about each other than that we were both feminists and writers with an interest in teen magazines, we were pretty sure that our shared love of *Sassy* meant that we were going to be similar in other ways as well.

And we were right. *Sassy* aficionados have always been a self-selecting group, people who wanted to establish a chosen community. "As someone who felt 'different' from a lot of other girls in my peer group, it was extremely validating to know that I was not alone in the way I thought or the types of things that I thought about," says fan Amelia Davis. *Sassy* still manages to function in this way, connecting people to one another. And while there were plenty of reasons for us to want to work on this book, the thought of meeting fellow *Sassy* fans, the friends we wished we would have had in high school, became increasingly exciting. It's embarrassing and kind of geeky—the idea that, as adults, we still believed that people who read *Sassy* would be like us, would have similar values and interests, and that, long after high school, finding these people would somehow still be transformative and fun and important.

But it was.

How
SASSY
Changed
My Life

· · · · ·

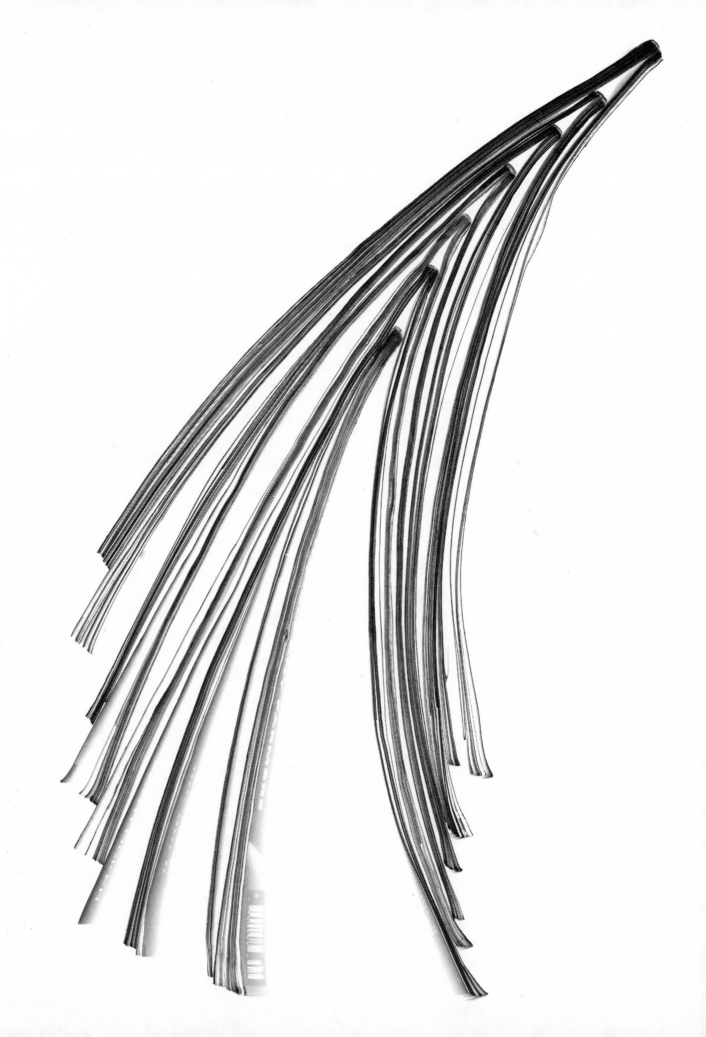

chapter 1

The Rise

b.s., or before *sassy*

Later, there would be the infamous Kurt and Courtney cover. There would be the R.E.M. flexidisc. There would be the seminal junk food taste-off and the first-person sex stories. There would be Jane and Karen and Catherine and Mike and Neill and Margie and Kim, and there would be Christina Kelly, regaling the world with stories of the menstrual cramps she endured while interviewing future talk-show hostess Rikki Lake. But before that, there was *Seventeen* magazine, and it regularly ran cover stories like "Bridal Sweet." "This was the day I'd always dreamed of," reads the copy. An accompanying photo pictures a beaming adolescent bride in her new husband's paint-splattered oxford shirt, eating takeout on the floor of their brand-new first apartment. But this wasn't 1957; this was 1987—three years after Madonna seduced a generation of teenagers by singing about premarital sex in a wedding dress.

Despite the fact that it was spinning its wheels in a different decade, *Seventeen* retained its place as the grande dame, the de facto how-to-be-a-teenage-girl guide. It was the nation's first teen magazine, and it hadn't veered from its civic-minded mission to create the world's most proficient wives since its debut, right after World War II. The magazine was essentially an etiquette guide for the all-American girl, doling out no-nonsense advice on appearances and relationships in between fawning celebrity profiles, home-decorating how-tos, and a parade of Nordic-looking models. Its owner, Walter Annenberg—a Nancy Reagan crony and millionaire with a gold-plated toilet seat in his private plane—called it "a national trust."

From the beginning, *Seventeen* practically invented the teenager as a category that could be marketed to, and the magazine lost none of its muscle over the subsequent forty years. Though it had spawned teenybopper wannabes like *YM* and *Teen*, its million-plus circulation and seemingly unassailable brand name made *Seventeen* the most coveted vehicle for advertisers. Big companies were convinced that if they could convert young consumers to their products, the girls' loyalty would remain after a walk down the aisle effectively ended their adolescence. Half of all *Seventeen* readers would graduate to the decidedly retro *Good Housekeeping* and the mildly liberated *Glamour* in their adult years, and they were a marketer's wet dream: soon-to-be happy homemakers and pink-collar office workers. They were the girls beguiled by the Jostens class-ring ad in the September 1988 issue, which featured a pretty young girl with a boyfriend's lips pressed to her cheek; the tagline reads "Guaranteed for Life."

But to achieve this promise of matrimonial

bliss—not to mention a spot in the homecoming court—there were a number of things a teenage girl needed to know, and to that end *Seventeen* served up dieting tips, recipes, and relationship advice. "High kicks and cartwheels aren't the only things that count in cheerleading tryouts. Appearance can make or break you, too," a beauty story admonishes. "Could you have possibly put on a few pounds over summer vacation?" worries one of the de rigueur diet articles. *Seventeen* could help: "Busy Bodies" features two girls and their editor-approved exercise routine.

Sure, there were plenty of things to worry about in high school: getting fat, wearing the wrong clothes, body odor. But *Seventeen* taught girls how to master these traumas, and once they did, they could participate in all kinds of teenage fun, like rushing a sorority or trekking to Florida for spring break—something, one article enthused, "you should do at least once." The beach, after all, was "hunk heaven." How to get one of these hunky guys? "Be patient, not pushy."

But *Seventeen* wasn't just invested in girls' present; it was also invested in their future. Nestled beside the ubiquitous ads for modeling schools, weight-loss camps, and "High School at Home in Spare Time" were blurbs for fashion-merchandising colleges and courses like "Learn How to Be a Secretary." The magazine's editorial component was slightly more ambitious, featuring regular stories like "How to Make the Most Out of Your College Visit." But lest you think that higher education was valuable for much more than getting a Mrs. degree, an article called "College Cool" from the August 1988 issue should change your mind. It's a greatest-hits list of "Wild Weekends," "What They're Wearing," "Where to Spy on Guys," and "Hot Dates." There's only one concession to academics: a severely truncated list of "Best Classes." Other articles for the aspiring coed (a word *Seventeen* used liberally and entirely unironically) include "Fighting the Freshman Fifteen: How Not to Eat Your Way Through the First Year of College" and a fashion story featuring students at Tulane, a school best known not for its academics, but for its parties.

Seventeen was most American girls' first piece of direct mail; 50 percent of them received the magazine. "Hillary Clinton read it when she was a teenage girl, and so did the girl who grew up to be a hairdresser," says Caroline Miller, who became the magazine's editor in chief in 1994. As such, its tastes were oppressively mass, with treacly profiles of mall queen Tiffany and hair band Nelson. It touted parentally approved entertainment in parentally clueless language: "It's the underage rage these days as adult dance clubs open their doors to the under-twenty-one crowd. Fruit juice flows and the music pounds as the younger generation rules the night!"

Typical *Seventeen* magazine fare included articles on how to write a check and how to handle a sudden downpour while driving. "Pizza: Have It Your Way" achieved *Seventeen*'s dual directives of teaching girls how to cook ("Read recipes to make sure you have the ingredients and understand the directions") while simultaneously making sure they didn't actually indulge in the fruits of their labor ("When ready for dessert, serve salad"). The magazine preached the middle-class ideals of common sense and moderation.

Seventeen's downmarket sisters were more of the same beauty, fashion, diet, celebrity, and trauma-rama stories, but half as sophisticated. *YM* and *Teen* paid breathless homage to high school's alpha males and featured mind-numbing articles like "Quiz: Are You Your Own Best Friend?"

hello, *dolly*

"The teen magazines here were like *Good Housekeeping* for teenagers, speaking with parental voices and looking like they were suspended in aspic," Sandra Yates, *Sassy*'s founder, told *The New York Times* in a 1988 profile.

In the early 1970s, Sandra was a single mother, just out of her teens, struggling to bring up two kids on a secretary's salary in Brisbane, Australia. It wasn't easy, but Sandra was used to that. She had grown up in poverty, left school at fifteen, and barely survived two disastrous relationships—both times, she lost her home. The only way she could make it, she figured, was by crawling up the corporate ladder. But the women's movement was just kicking into gear, and no matter how smart and ambitious they were, few females ever made it past the assistant level. But Sandra was an optimist. She was also a feminist. During her lunch break, she would abandon her typewriter, change into jeans and a T-shirt, and attend rallies for the Women's Electoral Lobby, the Australian equivalent of the National Organization for Women.

She hit some serious snags—a male manager who refused to have a woman working for him, another who made clear he would never promote one—but Sandra eventually landed an advertising sales manager position at one of Australia's premier newspapers. She worked with thirty men and one other woman—her secretary. Next she took a job, also in advertising, at Fairfax Publications, a big player in publishing, where she was quickly promoted to a top position. In 1987, Fairfax sent Sandra to New York City to investigate the company's potential to make its mark overseas. It was there that Sandra got the idea for *Sassy*.

Sandra thought American girls needed something different, something more like *Dolly*, the edgy, outspoken, Fairfax-owned Australian magazine. In other words, the *Times* reporter stated, "one that would discuss issues like sex, fashion, or suicide, without cloaking them in euphemisms, one that would take a tone of, in her words, 'Hey guys, we're in this together.'" *Dolly* ran stories like "Masturbation—It's Not a Dirty Word" and made fun of cross-eyed pretty girls in a story on model bloopers. It was the highest-selling teen magazine per capita in the world.

Sandra convinced her bosses that they should invest in her idea. She packed up her husband and kids, and she and her business partner, Dr.

Anne Summers (who had headed Australia's Office of the Status of Women and had written a book on Australian feminism), moved to New York. They immediately began putting their team together.

"I passionately believed that the key to *Sassy*'s success would be her very young staff," says Sandra. *Dolly*'s Australian employees were just a few years out of high school themselves, and this was evident in the way the magazine sounded. But the recruiting experience in the United States was difficult—"No one seemed to believe that we were genuinely expecting to hire a very young editor"—and firms kept sending much older candidates. The New York publishing world is a clubby, competitive place, and there was no dearth of corporate-clad, razor-taloned, senior-level editors who were ready to try their hand at the top slot of a brand-new, big-budget publication. But Sandra wasn't impressed by the usual suspects.

you *sassy*, me jane

Enter Jane Pratt, then just another twenty-four-year-old recent New York City transplant trying to make her name in the notoriously hierarchical publishing industry. But the relative newbie had impressed Marty Walker, who was helping Sandra with her search. Jane had worked with Walker at *McCall's* and was currently toiling at a struggling start-up called *Teenage*. Though she was young and inexperienced and didn't have a backer, she had begun telling people that she was starting her own publication for teens. "At the time, I thought I had labored so long," says Jane. "I had assisted, I had xeroxed, I had answered phones. It felt like, 'Damn it, it's time for me to have my own magazine.' "

As a lonely junior transfer to Andover—the elite prep school in Massachusetts that both her father and uncle had attended—Jane had devoured teen publications, trying to find girls like herself. "I just remember all these pictures of girls with tennis rackets, and they always had a boyfriend, and they all looked exactly the same," she says.

Jane was born in 1963 in Durham, North Carolina, the second oldest of four kids (two boys and two girls). Her parents were both art professors at Duke. Though she has said she was the "absolute worst" on the basketball team, she did well academically at the Carolina Friends School, a Quaker-run facility where there were no grades and no pressure. In fact, she started to get a little bored. So at fifteen, two years after her parents divorced, she left home for boarding school.

Right away she felt out of place on the preppy East Coast campus. "All of a sudden I was an outcast," she said in a January 1991 *Sassy* article called "When We Were Depressed." "The standards we were judged by were totally different. Being me wasn't enough anymore, and I had to give people specific reasons to like me—like being pretty or extremely smart or having money or a family who's somebody." She didn't really fit any of those criteria; in fact, her mom had gone

on unemployment briefly, and worked a paper route to support the family after the split. And it was hard to get to know the kids, many of whom had been boarders since they were in elementary school; no one was particularly interested in befriending the junior transfer.

But *Seventeen*, which Jane turned to for consolation, didn't exist to validate; it existed to proscribe. And it gave a lonely girl plenty of reasons to think her inability to fit in was her own fault. "Are you a bore?" asked one story that appeared during Jane's high-school years and preyed on young girls' deepest fears about themselves. "Your chatter may be driving friends away in droves."

"I felt completely disinterested in all the things I was supposed to be interested in," says Jane. "I held no passionate response to any of it, whether it was the pop stars being foisted upon me or the clothing that I was supposed to love to wear, or the kind of guys I was supposed to want to date and the kinds of things I was supposed to want to do with them on dates." In fact, dating itself seemed like a deeply foreign concept, yet another entrée into an inauthentic world. "The idea of dating was always like, 'Ugh! Gross!' To me, it just means that you are going to go somewhere and you're going to act like someone else, and it's tiring."

But there was no real place for Jane, who didn't feel that she fit into her high school's social strata. "It wasn't like I was so cool, like I knew about these bands that other people didn't know about and that I loved," says Jane. "*Sassy* was part of helping create those outlets for people like me. But at that time, there just weren't any." If she had been an adult, maybe she could have taken refuge in a feminist persona, listening to Joni Mitchell, reading Kate Millett, wearing hippie skirts, and letting her hair go gray. If she were a boy, maybe she could have been a punk, starting a band and dyeing her hair. But in the days before John Hughes peppered his oeuvre with smart, independent, not classically pretty, kind of freaky, kind of geeky, but also very cool girls who win in the end—though winning always means getting the guy—there were simply no role models.

She promised herself that if she ever got the opportunity, she would start a teen magazine for girls like her—girls who felt like they were outsiders, but who could still pass for normal in the high-school cafeteria. Girls who didn't want to completely reject mainstream culture, but didn't want to completely embrace it, either.

In the meantime, she wouldn't give up her destructive teen magazine reading habit. "I was addicted to them in a way, because of that terrible thing I think a lot of women's magazines do, which is to tear you down, but then tell you how they can help you fix yourself," she says. So one month *Seventeen* would run a guide on how to buy an engagement ring, and the next they'd run "Are You Really Ready For Marriage?"—a story about teen divorce. A story on how women spoil men too much is published just a few months apart from "Are You Too Assertive with Boys?" Jane would look to the magazine "to see what I should be, and when I wasn't, I would feel really bad. But I would think, 'Maybe through these pages I'll get some help, be more like those girls.' "

For a year, she was so stressed and upset that she practically stopped eating, and she started cutting herself. But the summer before her senior year, she became determined to change things. If she joined the cross-country team, she could go back to school two weeks early. She figured this would allow her to meet the other athletes and the new students, who she thought might be more open to her. So she trained all summer and got a new haircut, new makeup, and new clothes. It was exactly the kind of transformation that *Seventeen* would have endorsed; when she got back to school in September, no one recognized her. She had remade herself. "I had a great senior year," she said in *Sassy*.

After graduation, Jane matriculated to Oberlin, a small, liberal-arts college in Ohio, where she double-majored in English and dance, and where being a bit offbeat was prized, not denigrated. While there, she interned at *Style* and *Rolling Stone* and, afterward, at *McCall's*, before landing her gig at *Teenage*. Then she was called in to meet with Sandra Yates about a new teen magazine based on an Australian publication. She infamously showed up to her job interview in big black workmen's boots, a polka-dot skirt, and a vintage top. She looked, said Sandra, like she "got it."

"She asked me the craziest thing or wildest thing I had ever done, so I told her the story about when I met Michael Stipe," says Jane of her oft-repeated first encounter with the R.E.M. frontman, in which she chased down the van he was in as it left a club after a show. She had exams the next day, but "you know, whatever," says Jane, who could tell Sandra loved her response.

Jane seemed like the grown-up teenager Sandra was looking for. But Sandra wanted to make sure there was some substance to go with the style. She asked Jane if she gave money to any causes. Jane replied that she had given to the pro-choice organization National Abortion Rights Action League since she was a teenager. "I think that sealed the deal," she says. "I saw on her face, 'Okay, we got the girl.' " Sandra sent Jane to Sydney for six weeks.

sassy gets a staff

"She just sort of looked over the shoulders of everyone and asked us questions constantly," says Neill McCutcheon, *Dolly*'s art director, about Jane's time in Australia. "And you know, it was funny for us, because we were going, 'They hired her? Really?' "

If *Dolly*'s Australian staff wasn't yet quite convinced that the bouncy young American in miniskirts, anklet socks, and heels was right for the job, neither was Jane thrilled that she was inheriting a number of employees. Despite her exalted new job status, Jane didn't have complete control over staffing decisions. Sandra's boss had hired Cheryl Collins—*Dolly*'s former art director, who had spent the last eight months in the United States at *Mademoiselle*—to head *Sassy*'s art

department even before Jane was brought on board. Jane hired Neill as associate art director. Jacinta Dobson, *Dolly*'s Australian fashion editor, was also being shipped over to *Sassy*. Manhattan-born and -bred, RISD-educated Mary Clarke, who had toiled in the bland domesticity of *McCall's* (where she had recently been fired), and before that had worked at *Seventeen* (where she was scolded for wearing jeans and vintage clothes), was signed on as beauty editor.

Jane wasn't pleased to find out that one of the magazine's writers had already been hired. Karen Catchpole was a Californian who had skipped out on her last year of high school to move to Australia. She was working at a trade magazine about publishing and advertising, where her assignment was to write a story about Fairfax's launch of *Dolly* in the United States. "So I'm on deadline and I'm writing the story and I think to myself, 'That's where I want to work,' " says Karen, who had written exactly one freelance article—a profile of a male model—for *Dolly*. It was seven o'clock at night, but she called Sandra, who picked up. "I made some probably completely transparent pretext asking some question about the story, and then I basically just said, 'I want a job at this new magazine that you're doing,' " says Karen. There was a long pause. "Oh, yeah, you're American," said Sandra. Jane felt pressure to hire someone that Sandra liked, and, even though she was less than thrilled with Karen's ideas (Jane thought Karen's proposal to call the letters column Vox Pop was lame), hired her with the plan to "edit her like crazy."

Instead of arguing with her new boss, Jane concentrated on filling the remaining two writing slots. Jane had edited Catherine Gysin, an assistant with minimal writing experience, at *Teenage*. And though they weren't great friends, they had talked about *Dolly* and Jane's vision for the new magazine. Catherine was a midwestern girl who loved Yeats; had seen *On the Waterfront* thirty-six times; nursed a deep, abiding love for Sting; and was very close to her family. Jane thought Catherine was suited "to be the serious girl, the bookish kind of girl" the magazine needed. So she called Catherine late one night and offered her the job and a hefty raise. Catherine accepted immediately. "Being a staff writer was what I always wanted," she says. "I was thrilled."

There was just one slot left. A help-wanted ad in *The New York Times* had attracted a lot of prospective candidates, but most of them weren't very promising. It wasn't that they didn't have enough experience; plenty of people from publications that were both reputable and cool, like *Rolling Stone*, had met with Jane. But what Jane was looking for in a writer was "less about the way they wrote and more about the way they spoke, and their actual personalities." So far, no one had the right voice. She liked the way one cover letter that had come in was worded, but she kept bypassing the candidate, Christina Kelly, who certainly wouldn't bring any cool cred to the new magazine: Christina was an inexperienced writer who worked at *Footwear News*, a trade publication that covered the shoe industry in excruci-

ating detail. But Jane was getting desperate, so finally, with nothing to lose and without interviewing her first, she asked Christina to do an edit test, a mock version of a story she would write for the magazine. The topic: friends talking behind your back.

Elizabeth Larsen remembers the day they received Christina's test. Jane's new assistant, Elizabeth, had just spent three months in South America after graduating from Barnard. She, too, had answered a *Times* ad, though Jane's requirements for her position were notably less stringent. (Elizabeth claims she was hired for the boundless enthusiasm she showed for the magazine's prototype; Jane claims she was swayed by Elizabeth's resemblance to Shirley Temple.) "[The test] was what we would later recognize as vintage Christina. And Jane and I were looking at each other and being like, 'This is it!'" says Elizabeth. They were particularly impressed by a reference to pop princess Lisa Lisa of Cult Jam. "It sounded like a teenager speaks," says Jane. "It was perfect."

Jane called Christina in. "During my interview she was like, 'So what do you want to do?' and I was like, 'Um, I want to interview celebrities and cute boys,'" says Christina. It was the correct answer, but Jane was worried by how quiet Christina was in her interview—nothing like the attitude-filled article she'd written. So Jane had her come in again. Christina says she just knew that this was her ticket out of *Footwear News*. She called Jane "persistently, constantly, and then finally Jane was like, 'I have to get her off my back,' so she hired me."

the first issue

In October 1987, the full launch staff finally arrived at *Sassy*'s offices, located in prostitute- and peep show–infested pre-Giuliani Times Square— 1 Times Square, to be exact. Though there would eventually be desks in their pink cubicles, on the first day there were just typewriters strewn around the pink shag carpet. Jane's office had just recently been finished—it fit nicely into the color scheme, and was soon to be dubbed "The Pink Cave"—and everyone crammed in, arranging themselves on the floor for the first of many editorial meetings.

"I think we looked at *Dolly* and wanted to model ourselves after that," says Elizabeth. "But Jane had her own ideas."

There were plenty of *Sassy* columns—like the horoscope, quiz, and fiction sections, plus fawning profiles of no-name actors like Charlie Schlatter—that mimicked the usual teen-magazine fare. But there were many other aspects of the magazine that didn't resemble anything else in the genre, like "On the Road," which featured real kids—not models—talking about what's cool in their towns. (In the first issue, it's Miami.)

In the inaugural "Diary," a monthly note from the editor in chief, Jane is photographed wearing a T-shirt and denim jacket and, oddly, a faux Chanel baseball cap. She presents her persona as part hapless, part hip. "We're all still trying to figure out what being an editor in chief means," she says, then introduces each of her staff members, who appear again, just a few pages later, as reviewers for "Listen Up" (the record reviews) and "Watch This" (the movie reviews).

Jane wanted everyone to have a voice and used the magazine's first relationship article to establish her cast of characters. "It was a typical Wednesday-morning meeting," the piece opens. "Elizabeth and Catherine were having their usual argument over who's better-looking, Dweezil Zappa or Sting. Karen was cramming her second blueberry muffin into her mouth. And Jane had that I've-got-a-brilliant-idea look on her face. 'Why don't we do a story on how to flirt?' she said. 'Getting ready is the biggest part of flirting,' counsels Karen. 'I'm not admitting that I flirt, just that I think I'm good at it,' says Neill, in one of his earliest appearances as the magazine's resident lothario. 'I hate that word, *flirting*. It's such a giggly word,' says Mary derisively, adding that she never does it." Besides giving the reader a peek into how magazine stories are made, the piece's use of first-person journalism acknowledged that there wasn't only one way to flirt and that, in fact, it was totally acceptable not to partake at all—a potentially validating acknowledgment for the magazine's less sexually precocious readers.

The writers' voices were even apparent in their more serious pieces. "I caught the flu while working on this story. I gained five pounds and smoked a cigarette for the first time in a year," says Catherine in "Life After Suicide," a story about three teenagers who killed themselves and the devastating effect it had on their families. In a less grim but equally enlightening piece, "Backstage at Miss America," Catherine clued her readers in to the dark side of an event that teen magazines normally sold to girls as something to aspire to. "The judges have a complicated list of abbreviations that they write down next to each girl's name to keep track of the various body parts. For example, WC stands for weak chin. H means heavy. But my personal favorite is BB, which stands for big butt. Ah, the wisdom of the judges. As I overheard one judge say, 'This girl has to represent America. Someone with a big butt just doesn't do that for me.' "

The wink-wink, exasperated, bemused tone was completely unlike the vaguely disguised parental voice of *Seventeen* or the saccharine ditziness of *Dolly*. The writers and editors spoke to girls in their own language, which didn't come across as condescending or fake, since they were mostly in their early twenties themselves. In "Talk Behind Your Back," Christina's job-clinching story, her reader identifies with the heroine who is being ragged on by her friends. "You wonder what aspect of your personality has loosened the traitorous tongues of your friends, the wenches," she writes, sounding like Shakespeare's sister. Still not knowing what she's being shunned for—"Have you developed dandruff, severe acne, a nervous tic? Or is it your weight?"—

the beleaguered high-school student goes to class. Her hot English teacher informs the group that " 'Oscar Wilde once said that it is better to be talked about than ignored.' You derive some comfort from these words. More controversial people have said the same type of thing, including Madonna, who emerged from the mud bath of gossip a shining star." Christina invokes the totality of a teenage girl's world, in which pop-music divas, great dead white authors, best frenemies, and alluring adults figure equally. And she assumes they all get the joke.

Even better is that Christina conjures the real ambivalence of adolescence. At the end of the article she writes, "In college, I got into writing newspaper editorials stating that fraternities were sexist institutions that should be abolished (there were eleven fraternities at my school, all filled with good-looking guys). I was talked about pretty brutally by some of these guys, who thought I was weird. They also didn't ask me out much."

This level of honesty and intimacy was unprecedented in an American teen magazine. And both qualities were also particularly apparent in the magazine's first sex story. It's not that other teen magazines didn't cover this territory; *Seventeen* ran its clinical "Sex and Your Body" column every month. But in an article called "Losing Your Virginity: Read This Before You Decide," written by Karen, *Sassy* sounds more like a cool older sister than a high-school nurse.

Sassy looked as different as it sounded. All the other teen magazines were a mess when it came to art direction—unsophisticated and mostly black-and-white. *Sassy* was extra-wide and full-color from front to back. Still, photographers looked down on the idea of shooting for a new teen publication, and it was hard for the magazine to get the kind of top talent it wanted. But the design was in good shape; by the time Jane appeared at 1 Times Square, Cheryl had already put together a prototype, pages of *Dolly* with the *Sassy* logo added, which the sales staff was showing to prospective advertisers. It bore the brushed-ink logo that she had come up with one night because she wanted something handwritten. And the art department was happy, because for the most part, Jane left them alone. "You'd go to Jane and say what do you think and she'd say, 'Yeah, whatever you want, whatever you think,' " says Neill.

Beyond being pleased with her new boss's hands-off approach, Jacinta was excited by the American fashion establishment. "The clothes were so much better here. The models were better. Budgets were bigger," she says. In Australia, Jacinta had used lots of vintage because she didn't have access to big-name stuff. Here, she not only got to use the designer clothes, she got to go to the shows, too. "Betsey Johnson always gave us seats; Donna Karan wouldn't give us the time of day," she says. But it didn't matter because her mandate was to buck what was on the runway. Their shoots "had nothing to do with what was going on in the fashion industry. You could come up with things to start a trend." Jacinta, Cheryl,

and Neill worked closely on choosing models, but Jane retained final approval. She was looking for girls who would "be not model-y"—that is, a little off-kilter, not necessarily all-American.

To that end, "the cover was a big issue, trying to get the exact right feeling," says Christina. So, although the girl on the magazine's first cover is a blue-eyed blonde, her bandanna gives her a quirkier look.

On the last page of the magazine, there's a picture of a smiling, pixieish brunette, along with a note from Jane.

It goes like this: There was this great idea for a new magazine. But it didn't have a name. Well, actually the big guys who were putting it together had a whole list of names *they* liked—but whenever they asked anyone under the age of twenty-five, none of the names went over too big (to put it mildly). So one day, one of these guys went home and started explaining all of this to his daughter—thirteen-year-old Sara Walker. And she said, "Why don't you just name it *Sassy*?" Just like that. (Well, not just like that—the big guys then went and asked about two hundred more people her age what they thought, just to make sure.) So that's how *Sassy* was born . . . Oh. You want to know what some of the other choices were? Well, okay . . . things like *Chloe* and *Dawn* and *Amy* and *She* and *Me* and *Dee*.

Now aren't you glad Sara came along? So are we.

the response

The day the first issue of the magazine was being printed, Jane and Cheryl drove hours to visit the plant in New Jersey to see the cover and make sure it looked exactly right. "On the drive back, that was like the highest I've ever been in my whole life," says Jane. "We were giddy happy." It was partly exhaustion, but it was also a sense that they were on the verge of something new and important. Even though George H. W. Bush was favored to win the election—which didn't make the intensely liberal *Sassy* staff very happy—there was a sense that change was possible. Said Jane, "This is an amazing moment, because we could be doing something right now that could change the way an election could go! We're shaping these minds when they're really young. This is really important."

But the goal for the first issue was a little less ambitious: everyone just wanted it to sell. *Sassy* already had a small subscriber base. Charlotte Robinson was one reader who signed up for the first issue: "They got my name and address from *Seventeen* or some other shitty magazine I subscribed to and they sent me a big David Bowie poster with a description of *Sassy* on the back. Sold!" she says. But *Sassy* also needed to make a splash at the newsstand. Cover lines like "So You Think You're Ready for Sex? Read This First" and "Justine Bateman Speaks; Robert Downey, Jr., Freaks" did an

excellent job of reeling in thirteen- to eighteen-year-olds who saw it while grocery shopping with Mom or at the mall.

Becky Mollenkamp was thirteen when she bought *Sassy* in a Kmart because she loved the logo. "My friends all read *Glamour, Cosmo, Marie Claire*. I hated those things," she recalls. When she read *Sassy*, she says, "I just remember thinking, 'Finally, a magazine for me.' I wanted a magazine that spoke my language, discussed issues that were important to me, and made me feel special. *Sassy* did that. It was topics I cared about written in a, well, sassy voice, and it never seemed condescending. It wasn't a bunch of skinny models wearing expensive clothes and talking about how to please a man." Sarah D. Bunting's mom got her a subscription for her birthday and "my initial impression was that it was a trick—I was so used to the pink sparkly 'you're not allowed to sweat or get pissed off' *Seventeen*-speak that I couldn't quite believe it was a magazine for the same demo." Allison McPherson found it through a magazine fund-raising campaign at her high school in her small town (population 2,500). "I thought it was an exceptionally cool mag and I loved it from the start," she says. "With only thirteen other girls in my grade, I stuck out as the odd or desperately trying-to-be-original girl. I felt the rest of the girls were stuck in saccharine *Seventeen* or *Tiger Beat*." And "I was so excited that there was finally a magazine with a voice like 'ours,'" says Jen Hazen, who borrowed a copy from her high-school friend, loved the "funky" cover design, and read it cover to cover. "I was a subscriber to *Seventeen* at the time and was going through quite a rebellious stage, so it wasn't speaking to me. It felt too puritanical."

At least one *Seventeen* staffer agreed. "[*Sassy*] was like a lightning bolt," Annemarie Iverson, a beauty editor who later became her alma mater's editor in chief, told a *Mediaweek* reporter about the first time she saw the new magazine. "Everybody else felt the need to disparage it, but I felt terrible, like I was standing in my tracks. I missed something totally. It was a whole different voice and a different generation, and *Seventeen* suddenly felt antiquated to me—like it was a wearing a chastity belt."

chapter 2

The First Year

what's so sassy about *sassy*?

Shortly after the magazine hit news-stands, the mailman arrived at the *Sassy* office with a huge bag of letters. Jane and a few other staff members emptied the bag, sat on the floor, and read the letters one by one. "We couldn't believe how much our readers loved it and what they were saying," says Elizabeth, who was in charge of all reader mail.

Before *Sassy*, teen magazines pre-sented girls with two options: "Be like your parents want you to be, or like the boys want you to be," says Jen Hazen.

"Not: think for yourself. They didn't treat their readers like intellectuals." Or, in the words of Julianne Shep-herd, "It felt like the writers of *Sassy* were talking with me, rather than telling me how to be like more like them, or more like an idealized no-tion of the popular debutante teen."

Sassy was a refuge from airhead teenybopper magazines, and in its first two years, the magazine estab-lished its worldview. Girls weren't encouraged to be smart for the sake of getting good grades or getting into a good college. Instead, they were encouraged to be themselves. *Sassy* touted higher education's bastions of bohemia, like Oberlin, Evergreen,

Sarah Lawrence, and Colorado College, as well as all-female colleges like Bryn Mawr and Smith. An article called "These Are the Ten Sassiest Colleges in America," from the November 1989 issue, explains the list's criteria. Among them: "colleges that look for students who are die-hard individuals, creative, quirky, even," "education that is wide-ranging and free-thinking," "professors who encourage self-motivation and different points of view," "a tight, tolerant, nonelitest student body that is supportive rather than competitive," and "an emphasis on community service." It's as good a summary as any of what, in the magazine's microcosm, was important in the world, and what should be important to its readers.

It seemed like *Sassy* was trying to help its readers unlearn what they had learned in other publications. "I never got to go to Daytona Beach when I was in school . . . this major deprivation of my teenage years has really scarred me for life," Christina wrote in April 1989's "The Dirty, Scummy Truth About Spring Break (or, Where the Jerks Are)." In the article, she revealed the underbelly—including the drunk, assholish guys—of what had been sold to girls as a rite of passage. And in August 1989's "Cheerleaders as a Concept," she debunks the institution: "What bothers me is that it ultimately becomes this elitist activity where only the most 'popular' girls cheer on the most 'popular' guys. It's an outmoded system that stereotypes people. And that makes people like me feel inferior. Yeah. That's why I have a prob-

lem with cheerleaders. Not because they get more guys. I swear it."

Sassy questioned all the tenets that other teen magazines held dear. The magazine regularly made fun of celebrities; it exposed the tricks of the fashion industry in articles like May 1988's "How We Make This Girl Gorgeous"; it didn't deify models.

creating the characters

But what made *Sassy* really stand out was the way the magazine showcased its staff.

Sassy was cool in a distinctly impossible-to-focus-group way that was a direct result of the inimitable collective personality of the people who worked there. "When I hired the writers, I felt like I was casting a TV show, and trying to come up with characters so that every reader could relate to one of them," says Jane.

In the first year, she used her "Diary" column to familiarize readers with each staff member. *Sassy* introduced all of its writers and editors as specific archetypes with their own beats: after Jane, their fearless leader, there was Karen, the precocious straight-shooter who covered relationships; Catherine, the serious one who wrote the hard-hitting stories; and boy-crazy Christina. (Jane nicknamed her three writers "Sex, Drugs, and Rock 'n' Roll" for their respective areas of expertise.) But it wasn't just the writers whose personalities were known: Mary, for instance, was the cool, artsy one and Neill was the incorrigible flirt. "I wanted the hunky guy," says Jane of Neill's potential allure to readers and coworkers alike. "I made sure to get his picture in. He dated, like, half the girls on the staff. All the readers had crushes on him, and we would fight because sometimes he would get more reader mail than I would." (Some of the letters, he recalls, were quite suggestive.) Even Cheryl, who had no interest in appearing in the magazine, got dragged into a picture for the editor's letter about her, though only half of her appears in the frame. One can assume Jane thought the shy girls would relate.

Using the staff members as personalities in the magazine wasn't a brand-new idea. It had been done in small niche publications—mostly hunting and outdoors magazines—and it was a hallmark of *Dolly*, where employees would take turns writing the editor's letter. But though *Dolly*'s staff members sounded cool, they appeared at irregular intervals and were hard to differentiate. Jane decided to take the star system and ratchet it up a notch, giving the editors a real presence in the magazine, with lots of pictures, first-person stories, and references to one another. The staff would even interject the others' stories in countless parenthetical remarks. ("Once again I got the dream assignment," says Christina in a story on four up-and-coming male actors. "Yeah, we noticed," Karen and Catherine respond.)

Catherine had aspired to writing the entertainment articles, but quickly acclimated to her more serious beat, contributing some of *Sassy*'s most memorable stories, including a profile of an eighteen-year-old on death row and an article on a teenage stripper. While working on these pieces, she would go into "what we've come to know as 'Cath's serious obsession mode,'" as Jane described it in a December 1988 "Diary." Jane made sure to let readers know that, like those straight-A honor roll students who were reading, Catherine did her homework, including studying a 432-page tome on child preachers while writing her article "Children of God."

In an early issue, Jane introduces Karen, who was known for covering the fun, flirty side of being an adolescent girl, changing her hair color with every issue, and doling out important sex and relationship advice. The staff had an average age of twenty-four; Karen was the youngest, at twenty. Even though she was barely older than her target audience, she was known around the office for being wise beyond her years. "She has a motherly knack for putting things in perspective, like her multipurpose 'Who gives a flying ——,' used whenever Christina's worrying about what some celebrity will think of her interview or I'm deliriously murmuring that the magazine will never be done on time," wrote Jane. Plus, Jane says, she is "the only person I know—mothers included—who can talk about masturbation, boys' most intimate body parts, and the proper usage of each birth control method without blushing even once."

Christina's boy obsession was more libidinous than theoretical. In the early days, Jane portrays her as a kind of party girl. "No, Christina's not exactly camera shy. Or any kind of shy, really," says Jane in "Diary," noting Christina's "explosive laugh, which comes echoing out of her cubicle every, oh, fifteen seconds or so. And her 'Ohmigod!' squeal—you know, a la Moon Unit Zappa circa her 'Valley Girl' phase." Christina's main job was "getting to meet cute, famous guys and interview them." (Actors Billy McNamara and Alex Winter, and Kirk Pengilly—"the other cute INXS guy"—are a few examples.)

Readers got to know the staff so well that by the end of the first year, writers signed their stories with their first names only. True aficionados would read a *Sassy* story with the byline covered, then try to guess who had written it. The clues were so obvious, and the staff's personalities so defined, that it was hard to lose at this parlor game.

life at the office

As it is at almost any start-up—and certainly at a start-up where it's most of the staff's first or second jobs—the initial year at *Sassy* was chaos. Mary's boyfriend would come by and question whether anyone was actually working. Often, they were laughing at Andrea Linett, who, Mary says, is "the funniest person alive." The twenty-one-year-old Boston University graduate had started as the staff receptionist (she greeted Christina in striped over-the-knee socks, a baby-

doll dress, shorts, and Doc Martens). She spent the first few months smoking in the reception area and taking phone calls—or not: other staff members were constantly trying to hang out with her, and if she was deeply involved in one of their stories, she'd simply hang up on whoever called. She became the fashion assistant (and later the fashion editor).

But it wasn't just Andrea who provided office entertainment. Art assistant Danny Pfeffer would put on clothes that had been called in for shoots and catwalk through the office. Catherine says, "You'd try to think of reasons to go to the art department," where Neill blasted INXS from his cubicle (and mocked Catherine for playing *Les Misérables* in her own). Christina chattered on incessantly about a variety of male celebrities, addressed everyone (boys in particular) as "lovelamb," and paraded around in her wide-brim hats and "asking for it" micromini dresses ("I'd say, 'Christina, are you sure that's not a bathing suit?' " remembers Catherine). The time Eric Stoltz was in the lobby, a small parade of women walked by, one by one, trying to meet him.

Mike Flaherty, who was hired away from *Playboy* to be the copy editor in time for the fifth issue, was the only editorial staffer with a CD player, so he briefly hosted dance parties in his cubicle. If something amused Christina, "she'd just latch on to it and you'd hear about it every day," he says. So there was a "Low Rider" period during which six or seven staffers would groove to the War anthem for a few minutes each afternoon. "We were really into shtick," says Mike.

Even though everyone on staff was really different, "We were all close, and when we weren't working we'd go out together," says Elizabeth. There was a karaoke period. There was bowling. There was Nathan's and KFC for lunch. They even dressed alike: the summer *Dirty Dancing* came out, everyone in the office—except, presumably, Mike and Neill—started wearing three-quarter-length cutoffs and Birkenstocks. They also accused the less-cool kids—in this case, nerdier teen magazines—of copying them. They used words like *daggy*, Australian slang for *gross*, and published their definitions in the magazine, hoping they would catch on. (Alas, despite their valiant efforts to use it regularly in articles, you won't find *daggy* in the *OED*.) So though the staff often worked late into the evening, "We didn't notice the long hours," says Elizabeth. No one wanted to be anywhere else.

Certainly, there were cliques: the writers in their row of pink cubicles; the fashion department; the Australians—each had their own little circle. And there was a lot of personal drama, reminiscent of the volatile love lives of the teens they were writing about. Christina was in love with Neill, who was in love with Catherine. Elizabeth had a crazy boyfriend and was on the verge of joining a cult. Karen's marriage was ending. The staff was practically on top of one another. They could overhear one an-

other's phone conversations. There was a lot of crying.

They even lived together: Neill spent his first few months in the United States sleeping on Cheryl's couch. He later lived across the hall from Mary Kaye Schilling, the executive editor, a former *YM* staffer and dead ringer for Kate Pierson of the B-52's. She helped Jane with the day-to-day demands of editing the magazine. A promotional video shows them in their pajamas watching Sunday-morning cartoons together. Christina and Andrea moved in together. Jane lived across the street from Christina.

"Everything about the way we behaved was so adolescent," says Christina, who was, quite possibly, the biggest offender. "It was like something about dealing with the material of teenage life made us all act like teenagers."

But this was good for business. Some of the magazine's most popular stories covered life in the *Sassy* offices. In August 1988, the staff members switch jobs for a day. Karen finds out that copy editor "Anne's Job Sucks," while Anne wonders "Why Do I Have to Be Neill?" And "Cheryl promised that as art director I'd get to meet and talk to all the new boy models to decide if they should be in the magazine," says Christina. "But the old troll made me design the cover instead." The accompanying image shows the results, which includes headlines like "HUNK!"; "So You Want to Date a Rock Star?"; and "Nude Poster." Mary, filling in for Christina, forgets the questions she wanted to ask the pop group that she's interviewing, so "All we talked about were makeup and clothes!"

sassy is my friend

In the days before the World Wide Web and reality television, *Sassy* was like *The Real World* and a blog rolled into one: readers who picked up the magazine for an interview with their favorite celebrity or were titillated by a frank sex coverline kept buying it month after month because they wanted to hear from their favorite staff members. "I liked how personal it was," says Heather MacLean. "It was like a conversation with all these cool women every month." "It was like reading a long, loving letter from your big sis," says Max Weinberg. "It completely stood out from everything else, like there was actually a magazine out there that was designed for me," says Alicia Peterson, "written by people I wanted to know, featuring people I wanted to be, and seeming like it was made by friends. It was reassuring to know there were grown-ups out there who ended up doing something really cool with their lives and making an amazing magazine that meant something." Julie Gerstein agrees: "These girls were so snarky and witty and fun and you just knew that you would totally be friends with them if you lived in the same town."

The magazine got masses of letters. "They weren't 'Dear *Sassy*,' they were 'Dear Neill,' 'Dear Jane,' 'Dear Christina,' " says Jane. Most subscribers had a "writer crush," a *Sassy* staff member they most admired and emulated. It was the staff—not the actors or writers or models they covered—who were the stars.

Sometimes writing letters wasn't enough. Making a pilgrimage to the office and meeting the *Sassy* staff became a national pastime for readers. Peggy Lipton stopped by with her two *Sassy*-loving kids (by ex-husband Quincy Jones), Kidada and Rashida Jones, because Jane wanted to do a beauty story with the girls. "They sat in the art department with us and just sort of watched, and we explained to them what we did," remembers Neill. But it wasn't just famous people's progeny who got to hang out at *Sassy*. "Kids would come in all the time," says Neill. "And we made a point of being very open to it."

To a lot of readers, the *Sassy* staff was as important as—or more important than—their real friends. "I turned to the writers and editors, who I knew by name, for support when the boys in my language-arts class made fun of my pairing a big tweed coat with a short purple skirt and green tights," says Sarah Kowalski in an online *Sassy* eulogy. Millie di Chirico was just starting high school when she started reading *Sassy*. At that age, "The magazine was so personal it felt like a community, like people that you hung out with—that was very important. I was kind of an outsider type. I didn't have a lot of friends in school. You wanted to find your people."

Sassy, of course, vehemently dismissed the notion that the catty, claustrophobic, conformist halls of high school were as good as it got. The staff were candid about their own high-school horror stories, and by writing freely about their own adult lives—days spent hanging out with one another and with the various celebs who stopped by the office, nights spent at concerts—they implicitly assured their readers that adult womanhood was something to look forward to, and that though they were outsiders now, they'd be insiders eventually.

"We definitely felt like we really cared about the readers, and we didn't want to hurt them the way other evil magazines had, the way that had been done to us," says Christina. She adds, "The biggest dis on staff would be, 'That person doesn't really care about the readers.' " It was "a competition of who cared most."

"I think for a lot of the people who worked there, it had nothing to do with the glamour, the money," says Jane. "We didn't make any money, anyway. It was really just about these girls. We weren't faking that we wanted to be there for them, we weren't faking that we were their friends. We *were* their friends."

Though it was *Sassy*'s honesty and authenticity that readers responded to so strongly, in fact, the staff members' personas were at least partially just that: personas. Jane wanted characters in the magazine because that's what they had at *Dolly*, and she worked really hard on getting each character exactly right. She didn't want to change their voices, but to "enhance their voice, if anything. Tell them, 'Do more of that.' " Elizabeth says, "I think in a way it was hyperbolized." Certainly,

it wasn't made up. "I'm frighteningly well-adjusted," says Karen. "You would be horrified at how well-adjusted I am. I was very much the grown-up, sensible one." Still, she admits, "Did we hone in on one particular aspect of our personalities and really pump that up? Sure." Even Christina wasn't exactly as she appeared. In real life, she wanted more freedom to write issue-oriented stories, but her persona was all about boys and celebrities, so that's what she covered.

jane becomes a superstar

"People like Karen and Christina were really beloved by readers," says Mike. "They were like celebrities." But if Karen, Christina, et al. were merely like celebrities, Jane was the real thing. The *Los Angeles Times* called her "queen of the prom." "She's so *hot*," Quincy Jones told *New York* magazine. The media made much ado about *Sassy*'s young, charismatic, successful editor in chief, giving her full credit for the magazine's early success. "She really was good at developing a persona," says Mary Kaye Schilling. Jane was comfortable on television and being chauffeured around in cars. She always knew the right thing to say in interviews ("Now I'm the popular kid I wasn't when I was sixteen," she cooed to one reporter). During Jane's first month on the job, she had to prepare for one of many TV appearances. "She saw this suit that she wanted in a magazine, some pink suit, and she made Elizabeth call the designer to get it, find out where there was one in her size and have it delivered. And I thought, 'Who that young, in their first job, knows how to do that?' " says Mary Kaye. "I mean, she knew how to be a celebrity. And most celebrities know that instinctively, and none of us knew how to do that."

Jane was an extremely charismatic leader. "Story-idea meetings at *Sassy* were amazing," says Catherine. "Anything was possible. Jane made you feel like you could say the craziest thing in the world." In the first issue, there was an advertorial, the "prove how well you know *Sassy* contest." Jane asked Elizabeth to write the paragraph of copy, her first piece of real writing, and she sat at the typewriter sweating, working on it for an entire day. Elizabeth handed it in as Jane got in a car to catch a flight. "She called me from the airport, saying, 'I love it, it's perfect,' " says Elizabeth. Though she would often make the writers go through as many as fifteen story drafts, she was careful to keep the authenticity of each of their voices. And she made each of them feel valued, littering their copy with lots of checkmarks and *ha!*s. She was also careful to let the rest of the staff know how good they were at their jobs.

And she ran the office like *Dolly* and other Australian magazines were run, which meant "it was not hierarchical at all. It was a very small staff, and it was very loose," Jane says. But being a media darling wasn't always easy in such an egalitarian office. "She was in an interesting position," Elizabeth says of Jane. "She was younger than everyone but me and Andrea. She was very supportive, but had a very strong idea of what she wanted." She was also juggling a lot of different duties. According to Elizabeth, "She not only had to put together the magazine, she had to sell the magazine, and she had to sell and market herself as a personality." Each day was divided between endless meetings with Sandra, or the business side, or the editorial team, or the art department. "There was no moment of her day that was unaccounted for," says Elizabeth. "She barely got in a snack."

None of this was easy for a twenty-four-year-old. "The creative part of it seemed very natural; I knew exactly what I wanted," says Jane. She had never managed anyone other than an intern before, and now she was managing a whole group of people, some of whom were twice her age. In June 1988, just six months after the staff had officially started work, they all went to Sterling Forest in upstate New York for a staff retreat. It was supposed to be like camp. It began as a strategy meeting–cum–bonding session, with everyone making presentations on their positions. ("We had this room, and I had to stand up in front of everybody and talk about how I was going to tailor punctuation and grammar to the *Sassy* voice. And I remember just wanting to die," says Mike, on his copyediting presentation.) But the retreat quickly devolved as staff members confronted Jane about a litany of small problems at the magazine. (They couldn't have been too monumental, since no one seems to recall the specifics.) At one point, in the midst of hanging out, Jane had a panic attack and broke down sobbing. She finally had to leave.

"We used to fight like crazy," says Neill, who, by all accounts, orchestrated the mini-mutiny. "We were allowed to; it was the structure. Everyone had a voice, and when everyone has a voice, it's mayhem."

chapter 3

Feminism

ms. junior

· ·

Ragon Duffy went to pro-choice rallies in her stroller and was the only sixth-grader in town with a KEEP YOUR LAWS OFF MY BODY button on her backpack. Her mom bought her a subscription to *Sassy*. "Which was particularly cool, since she wouldn't buy me any typical magazines at all," says Duffy. "We were a feminist household: no Barbies because she was bad for body image and self-esteem; not a lot of TV or pop-cultural things; lots of books." But Duffy's mom read about *Sassy* in *Ms.*

magazine and decided to give the little sister of feminism's standard-bearer a try. Duffy liked the publication for more than its politics. "I loved it because it was a magazine just for me. It had a certain snarky sense of humor. And it was all about how it was cool to be different and to just be who you are," she says. "I was the geeky, shy older daughter and while my mom was a very cool person, I didn't think she understood the stresses and influences in my life." *Sassy* did.

Sassy's reliance on personal stories and truth-telling were very much in the feminist tradition; so was its emphasis on choice and the politics of daily life. Its tone was equally important. Duffy liked that *Sassy* talked about its subjects in "a non-patronizing way." Plus, "I liked that its articles focused on girls as people and always emphasized how much power you could have."

At first, *Ms.* seemed like a funny place to carry an ad for a teen magazine that heralded celebrities, makeup, fashion, and cute boys. *Ms.*, which was founded in 1972 to be the mouthpiece of the then-burgeoning Second Wave of the women's liberation movement, had a reputation for refusing to cozy up to any of those topics, preferring to focus on political, legal, and socioeconomic issues like war, sexual harassment, and breaking through the glass ceiling. *Ms.* was supposed to be an alternative to the softer, more conciliatory "Seven Sisters"—the industry name for recipe-, fashion-, and marriage counseling–heavy women's titles like *Ladies' Home Journal, Family Circle,* and *McCall's.* Because *Ms.* refused to offer "complementary copy"—stories to make you want to buy the products in the publication's ads—the magazine remained a struggling not-for-profit until Sandra Yates came along.

"I'm going to prove you can run a business with feminist principles and make money," Sandra told *The New York Times* in 1988. In the beginning, she did. *Sassy* had been on the market for just a month when Fairfax decided to divest its U.S. properties by April of that year. Sandra and Dr. Anne Summers joined forces to create Matilda Publications and bought *Sassy* and *Ms.* in only the second leveraged buyout in U.S. corporate history

to be led by women. "I think there was definitely this idea that *Sassy* would be this sort of prep school for future *Ms.* readers," says Karen. The pair led *Ms.* to its highest-ever circulation at 550,000; *Sassy*'s circulation was soaring as well.

The *Sassy* staff was excited by the new relationship. By and large, they had grown up with feminist *Ms.*-reading mothers. Jane listened to *Free to Be You and Me* as a kid; she and her mom marched in support of the ERA. Christina's mom "was what my father calls a 'Women's Libber,' " she recalls. "But she was a suburban mom. She was no Betty Friedan." Neither was most of the *Sassy* staff. But if they weren't activists, waving placards and conducting sit-ins like the women at *Ms.*, they had grown up reaping the benefits of the women's movement. They went to college at a time when women's studies departments were on the rise, priming them to think that anything was possible, and that there was nothing more normal than to deconstruct gender roles.

But despite a shared owner and political impetus, "The *Ms.* and *Sassy* people didn't really interact," says Jennifer Baumgardner, who started working at *Ms.* in 1992 and, as the publication's youngest staff member, was one of the few to befriend the teen-magazine editors. "The *Sassy* people were very intimidated by the *Ms.* people because we were supposedly the intellectual and serious feminists. And the *Ms.* people were intimidated by the *Sassy* people because they were stylish and knew Michael Stipe."

But even if the *Sassy* staff never felt embraced

by their feminist elders, the sight of Gloria Steinem in the communal bathroom was still a thrill. Did they look up to the activists across the hall? "Absolutely, yes," says Karen. "But then I think we were doing our own thing. I think we recognized that the language that they were using wouldn't be right for our readers."

And *Sassy* had to do their own thing if they were going to reach young girls. Feminism had a persistent PR problem, and not just among teenagers. Throughout the eighties and nineties, mass media continued to portray the women's movement as a crusade led by a few angry, man-hating women to bring down the family, the economy, and American life as we know it. A 1989 *Time* magazine article claimed that "to the young, the movement that loudly rejected female stereotypes seems hopelessly dated." And while *Time* is guilty of frequent exaggerated declarations that feminism is dead, it's true that by the time *Sassy* readers were in high school, the Second Wave's consciousness-raising sessions—women-only get-togethers during which they traded truths about their lives—seemed hopelessly dorky. In a way, a commercial magazine with advertisements for eye shadow and Doc Martens was the perfect place for the *Sassy* staff to get out the message that girls were equal to boys, that the right to abortion was imperative, and that being smart was more important than being popular. *Sassy* was like a Trojan horse, reaching girls who weren't necessarily looking for a feminist message.

the early sex stories

In some ways, *Sassy* defined itself by what it was not: no diets, no fawning coverage of teenybopper celebrities, and no talking down to its readers. But there were other areas that deserved a more proactive approach. Since the publication of *Our Bodies, Ourselves*, the women's movement had sought to educate women not only on sexual health, but on pleasure as well. The magazine's most obviously feminist-minded content that first year was sex education.

At the staff's very first editorial meeting, the editors universally agreed that providing their readers with sex education was a top priority. Says Karen, who penned the majority of the sex stories, "We knew—because we weren't that far from the demographic ourselves—that there was this real world of people under the age of nineteen and sex." Meaning, they were having it. "And then there was this shiny, pretty, sweet-smelling teen-magazine world" that tried desperately to pretend like that wasn't happening.

Sexual mores were changing drastically in the late 1980s, and girls weren't having an easy time of it. The more casual attitude toward sex fostered in the sixties and seventies had fully permeated the culture, but the idea that you could have premarital sex if you wanted to transmogrified into the idea that you *should* have premarital sex, if you wanted to be cool. And in the home-alone era of latchkey kids, adolescents were spending more time than ever unsupervised. By the time of *Sassy*'s debut, a girl trying to negotiate the slippery slope of adolescent sexuality was pretty much on her own. "Adults weren't around, and they had no protection culturally," says Caroline Miller. "They couldn't say, 'My dad will kill you, it's a sin.' If a guy came on to you and you didn't want to have sex, you had no ammunition except 'I don't want to.' And you have to be very mature to say to a guy, 'I don't want to.'" A lot of girls didn't know if they wanted to or not: How do you weigh concerns about your reputation against concerns about your own desire against concerns about alienating a potential love interest? Every sexual encounter was fraught with choices. "The patriarchy went away and we abandoned these thirteen-year-old girls and they really were, to some extent, without weapons in the arsenal," says Miller.

And yet the specter of being called a slut was as strong as ever. (Many girls were so ambivalent about sex that they allowed themselves to be "swept away" by romance rather than plan for the loss of their virginity—the subject of a September 1987 story in *Seventeen*. Another story was titled "When You've Gone Too Far.") The simultaneous pressure on girls to have sex and to not have sex was a terrible double-bind. From 1970 to 1988, according to the Centers for Disease Control, the share of fifteen-year-old girls who were "sexually active" rose from 5 to 25 percent; among nineteen-year-olds, the share rose to 48 percent.

Certainly, pop culture was no help. "We felt at least one reason so many teens were having sex was that the media had successfully convinced them that losing their virginity would be the biggest moment of their lives," reported Elizabeth

in an article she later wrote for the *Utne Reader*. In fact, *Seventeen*, *Risky Business*, Madonna, and countless after-school specials were arguably implicated in the sexual confusion that ran rampant among teenagers. By making intercourse seem like such a big deal—whether by insinuating that it should only be whispered about in hushed tones or that it was the raison d'être at Friday night's kegger—the importance of a teenager's sexual status was blown way out of proportion. In Jane Austen books, the characters talk constantly of marriage; on MTV and in John Hughes movies, the chatter is always about sex. But while the generation weaned on erotically charged pop culture was more familiar with innuendo than were previous generations, there was still plenty of confusion as to how to prevent pregnancy and STDs.

Since the late 1960s, when Helen Gurley Brown introduced the notion of the sexually voracious Cosmo Girl, frank sex talk had been a frequent subject in women's magazines. Even in teen magazines, sex education was a staple, but it was dealt with in clinical language; an undercurrent of fear and foreboding prevailed. In the late 1980s, AIDS was being used as a scare tactic to get teenagers to remain abstinent. But clearly it wasn't working; the United States had (and still has) the highest teen-pregnancy rate in the Western world. The *Sassy* staff knew there was a void in their readers' sex education.

"Even without an orgasm, sex can be enjoyable," was just one of the facts in the premier issue's "Losing Your Virginity" article. The piece offered anonymous accounts of various girls' first times, some with serious boyfriends, some with one-night stands. According to Elizabeth, *Sassy*'s strategy was to "provide more realistic accounts and leave the moral up to the teen." For the piece, "we hunted down some of the most burning questions (you know, the type that make even Madonna blush) and found the answers for you." It wasn't exactly the teen version of *Cosmopolitan*; the article answered clinical questions like "When do most girls and boys lose their virginity?" and "How should I guard against pregnancy, AIDS, and other sexually transmitted diseases?" and those with more emotional resonance like "Should I talk during sex?" and "How long will it take?"

But *Sassy* wasn't completely immune to re-hashing the usual sex-ed lesson, as evidenced when Karen assured readers that "Love and sex go together." But she went on to put her own personal twist on it when she further noted, "Sure, they exist separately, but they're better together (believe me)." "Many couples consider foreplay an important part of sex—even an alternative—and use it to extend and enhance sex . . . It's a good way to relax and become stimulated—especially the first time, when you're likely to be nervous already," advised the magazine, which also recommended using a lubricant if you're worried about intercourse being painful. The concept that girls could derive anything but discomfort and awkwardness from their first sexual encounters was unlike anything in any teen magazine prior (or since), and the idea that girls could—and should—enjoy sex, educate themselves about sex, and talk about sex was a distinctly feminist notion.

In *The Wall Street Journal*, Sandra says that the first issue's articles, including the sex-ed story, were researched intensively in focus groups. "The teens," Sandra reported, "said their parents would be happy for them to be getting that information, and glad they wouldn't have to do it themselves." They were probably right: although 65 percent of American parents reported that they were in favor of comprehensive sex education that included information on birth control, the number of high schools that taught this kind of information (or, according to a 2001 Alan Guttmacher Institute report, "controversial" subjects like abortion and sexual orientation) decreased dramatically after Ronald Reagan signed the Adolescent Family Life Act in 1981. Instead, the federal government began investing in local programs to prevent teenage pregnancy by encouraging chastity and self-discipline.

Elizabeth recalls the office being flooded with feedback on "Losing Your Virginity" and for the frank "Help" column, which she edited. "I read all the reader mail, and I knew that there were a lot of dark things happening," she says. "We got horrifying letters about incest. We got sweet, enchanting letters like, 'My sister has more breasts than I do.' They were grammatically incorrect, with smiley faces over the i's. But they were about girls being pressured to have sex, cutting themselves, throwing up every day after they ate. On little lined notebook paper we'd get tons and tons of mail." It was clear to the *Sassy* staff that they had hit a nerve. Beyond a very real lack of information and resources, Elizabeth wrote in *Utne*, "what was most disconcerting for us was the fear and shame these letters portrayed."

Sassy made an effort to address its readers' most persistent issues. In June 1988, an article titled "Getting Turned On" answered questions like "What Makes It Happen?" "What Does It Feel Like?" and "Am I Weird If I Don't Feel It?" The answer to the last one was "No. Neither are you a weirdo if you have constant daydreams about sex with Brian Bloom. (Well, if your fantasies are about Brian Bloom, you're walking a fine line.)"

The article ends on a typically *Sassy* note: "The key to understanding your own sexuality is knowing what you are—and aren't—ready for. Maybe you're ready to take your sexual feelings a step further by masturbating or having sex. Or maybe you're content with your Brian Bloom fantasies. Either way, remember there is no 'right' decision—except the one that you feel ready for."

In addition to covering sexual health, *Sassy* also covered sexual orientation. In the second issue, the magazine ran an article titled "My Best Friend Died of AIDS," which covered the life and death of a gay teenager. In July, *Sassy* tackled the issue of homosexuality again. "Laural and Lesli and Alex and Brian are your basic kids. They're dating. They go to movies and concerts. They fight over stupid things. They make up. They're sad sometimes. They're happy. And they're gay," the tagline read. The piece portrays the two college-age couples as totally normal kids who love each other, struggle with parental disapproval, and go to B-52's concerts. " 'Straight

people are always asking "What do you do in bed?" ' says Alex. 'Who says we even go to bed?' " And though there's some wink-wink sexual innuendo—" 'We like doing physical things together,' Laural says. 'Yeah,' Lesli says, raising her eyebrows lasciviously. 'Besides that,' Laural says, slapping her hand"—the piece focuses mostly on their relationship, not their sex lives. "The whole time Lesli is talking, Laural is holding her hand. These two are solid, stable," writes Catherine.

But the piece also included some points that were probably harder for a lot of parents to swallow, like when Laural says, "You can have feelings for a woman or even make love to a woman once and it won't necessarily change your life; I mean, you won't necessarily be a lesbian." Or when Alex complains that in suburbia, he is taunted with cries of, "You homo, you fag, you AIDS victim."

Despite advertisers' concerns about *Sassy*'s sexual content, the magazine was an immediate business success. It scored ads from Benetton, ArtCarved class rings, Cover Girl, and even Trojan condoms, making *Sassy* the first American teen magazine to accept condom ads and proving that its commitment to sex education extended beyond its health features. But the loving, humanistic portraits of gay teens made the already skittish advertisers increasingly nervous. "Sandra and Jane spent a lot of time educating them about why it was important to talk to teens this way and do these stories," says Elizabeth. "Advertisers would say, 'Okay, we'll try it out, take you at your word.' "

the boycott

As the first new teen magazine to come along in years, *Sassy* was getting its fair share of attention beyond the magazine industry. Sex stories made a particularly easy subject for the news media to grab onto. Jane was on a national media tour, going city to city and doing local TV, and was often asked whether the question "Are you ready for sex?" was promoting teen experimentation. In the article of the same title, Karen wrote about practicing rolling condoms on a banana. "Even that—which doesn't seem like that big of a deal—people were already starting to watch us then," says Jane.

And, naturally, not all of these people were pleased. Irate parents called *Sassy*'s office to complain; some canceled subscriptions. Perhaps even liberated, formerly free-loving, *Cosmo*-reading, baby boomer parents weren't always as comfortable with the concept of teenagers and sex—or the idea that their daughters didn't need to ask permission to lead their own erotic lives—as they thought they were.

In fact, the country was deeply divided about the place of the patriarchy in the lives of teenage girls: the death of Becky Bell in 1988—from the complications of an illegal abortion, which she underwent rather than tell her parents about her pregnancy and ask for consent for a legal procedure—was a lighting rod for abortion-rights groups, who blamed Indiana's parental consent law, and anti-abortion groups, who blamed the country's flimsy moral fiber. Jan Dawes—the mother of three sons, all grown—was in the latter camp. The woman from Wabash, Indiana, together with two of her Christian girlfriends, launched a petition campaign against the magazine. And she convinced her local Kmart and Hooks Drug Store to stop stocking *Sassy*.

Dawes was a member of a right-wing group called Women Aglow. The organization, which still exists today, is a proponent of laughably misogynistic beliefs. In an article on their Web site titled "10 Things Men Need to Know About Women," item number six is "I need your logical, objective perception of things as much as you need my intuitive, subjective sensitivity. I get so emotionally involved in situations that I don't see it clearly." Item number eight is "I really do want you to be my spiritual leader."

In the late 1980s, the religious right was just beginning to gather steam—*The Silent Scream*, a movie condemning abortion, was being screened to young pregnant women—and targeting teen-agers was a priority. Other like-minded organizations saw what Dawes was doing and decided to join her anti-*Sassy* crusade. In July, Focus on the Family, a California-based group headed by conservative activist James Dobson—who would later become known for having the ear of Karl Rove, George W. Bush's chief of staff, and loudly and successfully crusading against gay marriage—published an article in the *Citizen*, the group's monthly newsletter, denouncing the magazine as "without question the most sexually provocative teen magazine ever published."

In America, at least, this was probably true. While *Seventeen* had at least one article pertaining to sex every month, most of *Sassy*'s early issues contained more sexual content. The May issue may have been particularly interesting to hormone-addled adolescents. In addition to "She Was a Teenage Stripper" (hardly a how-to), there is "What Your Mom Doesn't Know About You" ("Wow. Only 14 percent of mothers thought their daughters had lost their virginity . . . But c'mon, moms, this is 1988") and "How to Kiss" ("Do put your fingers in his mouth. Okay, I was forced to put this one in. A few sickos—I mean people in this office—brought it up and I must admit there have been a couple of guys in my past who have gotten into it"). The "Help" section includes a letter from a girl who is having sex with her female friend and wants to stop, and one from a girl who has a teacher who "wants to jump on me." There's also a "What Now" piece bemoaning the fact that ten states are instating parental consent laws for girls under eighteen who want to have abortions.

But the article that so rankled Dawes, which was published in the second issue, was called "The Truth About Boys' Bodies." She told Dobson: "Let me just say that I've been married for thirty-one years. There was information in that particular article that I found offensive and shocking. And, having had a fulfilling relationship with my husband for thirty years, it was information I could well have done without." But it's hard to imagine that a woman who lived with four males wouldn't already be familiar with the article's con-

tents. There wasn't a particularly pornographic element to the high-school health-class basics that *Sassy* was presenting; it was mostly highly uncontroversial facts, like "at about age fourteen, a guy's voice changes from something that sounds like Pee-Wee Herman to something that sounds more like John Wayne (he hopes)." In one section, titled "Below the Belt," Karen writes, "You can't fool me. I know you're all reading this section first." And while she goes on to use the words *testicles*, *pubic hair*, and *penis*, it's still science-textbook chaste. The cheekiest part of the article is the cartoon illustration of a dorky-looking dude clad only in heart-covered boxers, accompanied by a few sentences debunking the old wives' tale that the shape and size of a boy's fingers are related to the shape and size of his penis—"So you can stop staring at that guy in chemistry with the huge hands."

In the *Citizen*, Dobson enumerates a number of other articles he finds offensive, including "Swimsuits We Dare You to Wear," a "Condom Update," and the "What Now" about parental consent before obtaining abortions. Thumbing his nose at the ninth commandment, he also listed pieces that were blatant fictions: stories titled "Good Manners for Good-Mannered Sex," "Seductive Nights: Daring Designs That Will Make Any Night a Night to Remember," and "Snakes and Lovers" (what is *that*?) never ran in the magazine.

But Dobson's piece wasn't meant to be descriptive—it was a call to action accompanied by a "What You Can Do" sidebar, which directed angry acolytes to make their displeasure known. Dobson kindly included a list of who's who to complain to, and their addresses. Besides Jane Pratt, it included Revlon, Noxell (owner of Noxzema and Cover Girl), Schering-Plough, Inc. (Maybelline), Carter-Wallace Inc. (Nair, Sea & Ski tanning lotion), and Tambrands, Inc. (Tampax, Maxithins). In other words, all of *Sassy*'s biggest advertisers.

Hundreds of letters poured into the 1 Times Square offices. In response, Jane dutifully published a letter in the *Citizen* that read "*Sassy* in no way intends to take the place of parents or to undermine their values. We only hope to be a source of entertainment, companionship, and information for teenagers at a time when such information is potentially a matter of life and death . . . In the end, our goals are probably not so different."

But if Jane and her staff weren't particularly concerned by Dobson, they soon had Reverend Donald Wildmon, the head of the American Family Association, to contend with. Wildmon had already launched a successful advertising campaign against the TV raunchfest *Married with Children* when he began publishing articles criticizing *Sassy* in his bulletin, which reached millions. And the Moral Majority launched their own campaign, claiming that *Sassy* promoted sex and homosexuality, and that its stories threatened parent-child relationships.

With three right-wing groups on the attack, letters from parents and other concerned zealots flooded into the offices of Procter & Gamble, Tampax, and the like, threatening the companies that they would lose customers if they continued to advertise in *Sassy*. Within a matter of months, *Sassy* had lost nearly every ad account. To put it another way, the magazine's debut issue was 129 pages; in April 1988, the magazine was 105 pages; and the following month it was 97 pages—a result of decreasing ads. According to the February 1989 issue of *Adweek*, twelve newsstand chains stopped carrying the magazine.

The staff jokingly referred to the magazine as the "*Sassy* pamphlet." But the business repercussions were hardly laughable. "We basically had, like, Guess Jeans as our only advertiser. Maybelline pulled out. Cover Girl pulled out," says Mary. "I have to appreciate Paul Marciano of Guess Jeans," agrees Jane. "He came to *Sassy* because of the controversy."

The same thing that got Guess on board with *Sassy*—it made good business sense for a brand with a risqué reputation—kept advertisers with more wholesome images away. It was hardly a moral decision. Though advertisers' unwillingness to support *Sassy* was blamed on the magazine's sexual content, Elizabeth wrote in *Utne*, their concerns were really about sales. "I realized that many of the same companies that objected to 'Sex for Absolute Beginners' in *Sassy* nevertheless advertised without complaint in *Dolly*—the most widely read teen magazine in the world in terms of circulation per capita." (In fact, *Dolly*'s sex education stories could make Dr. Ruth blush: "An old man wanking in public is a dirty thing," advised one on the do's and don'ts of masturbation.) But mass-market companies are intrinsically skittish.

They didn't necessarily think that what *Sassy* was saying about sex was wrong; they simply didn't want to rock the boat and anger any of their potential consumers. It was safer for them to place their ads in less controversial magazines that wouldn't upset an increasingly vocal constituency.

"There was a kind of sexism back then. Advertisers didn't really believe girls had money and, if they did have money, they really felt like they only understood makeup," says Sarah Crichton, who was executive editor of *Seventeen* at the time. In the late 1990s, companies started to see that girls had lots of disposable income, and they were spending it on all kinds of things—fashion, cars, gadgets. But in the eighties, it was a struggle "to convince advertisers that teenage girls had any impact financially at all," Crichton says. Clearly, keeping girls' parents happy was more important than impressing young consumers.

Something was going to have to give. And that meant editorial compromise. The September issue was already being printed when a story debunking the myths of masturbation ("maybe you call it jerking off, a hand job, beating off") was deemed too risky and was pulled. "A big advertiser said, 'If you run that story, we will pull all of our ads.' And we literally stopped the presses and replaced the story with something else," says Karen, who authored the story. She adds that in her rage, she "was throwing things." (She later gave the story to riot grrrl zine *Girl Germs* to publish.) So many companies were pulling ads out of the magazine that no one staff member can remember exactly which one delivered the final ultimatum on the piece.

There was also one other matter. A reader had sent in a question to the "Help" column asking if she could get AIDS from giving her boyfriend a blow job. It was one thing to say "oral sex"—*Seventeen* certainly did—but Sandra Yates thought the colloquial phrasing would add more fuel to the fire, endangering the magazine's existence.

"The language just bothered people, because it was that thing that *Time* magazine called 'Pajama-party journalism,' " says Jane, referring to the informal way *Sassy* spoke to its readers. "To use that language when you're talking about sex made these old men at the ad agencies feel like we were encouraging it somehow. But we weren't; we were just talking about it the way kids talk about it. They didn't understand half the words we used, and that made it hard. 'So you're promoting blow jobs.' No, we're not promoting them, we're saying you could get AIDS from them."

The "Help" page of that issue had to be shredded.

"If they had produced the issue as it was, they would have been on their way out of business," Michael Drexler, the national media director of the Bozell ad agency, told Jonathan van Meter in an article he wrote about the boycott for *7 Days*, a New York City weekly. "No question. The end."

underestimating the enemy

Before the boycott, "I don't remember her stopping us from doing anything," says Jane of Sandra. And though she occasionally vetoed ideas because they were too expensive, "She never vetoed anything on the basis of it being too crazy or wild, ever."

A quintessentially Australian publisher, Sandra really believed in letting her young staff make the editorial decisions. And why not? In less than six months from its launch, *Sassy*'s circulation climbed from 250,000 to 500,000, making it one of the most successful women's magazine launches in history. And though Sandra was business-savvy enough to pull the masturbation and blow-job stories at the crucial eleventh hour, in some ways, it was too little, too late. In fact, she had never really understood the dire threat the right wing posed. No one from Australia did. "I couldn't believe it. Neill was the same," says Cheryl. "The things we were writing about—relationships, suicide, masturbation—we had run in Australia without a problem."

When the boycott started, "Sandra was amazing," says Elizabeth. "She said, 'Let's stay the course. We will educate the public about this.'" In many ways, her cultural naïveté was what helped make the magazine so special.

Jane and Sandra embarked on a cross-country tour to try to pacify advertisers and wholesalers, to tell them why *Sassy* should be back on newsstands. They certainly had the blessing of the industry. "Both the Magazine Publishers of America and the American Society of Magazine Editors were very supportive of *Sassy* when the boycott began," says Sandra. Support came from a few other unusual sources as well: Kevyn Aucoin, the late celebrity makeup artist, was working

with Cover Girl at the time, and told the company he would stop unless they reinstated their ads. "I didn't find this out until later," says Jane. "He called them and said, 'I'm not going to work with you guys anymore unless you put your ads back in *Sassy*,'" He knew that their pulling out was related to the articles the magazine had run on homosexuality, and "he thought that it was amazing, what we had done."

For the most part, Sandra and Jane's plan worked. Though *Sassy*'s first publisher, Helen Barr, quit—aghast at the magazine's continued pushing of the proverbial envelope—a new publisher was hired, and advertisers slowly came back. *Sassy* even tried to make peace with Women Aglow, doing an "On the Road" on Jan Dawes's hometown of Wabash, Indiana. ("It did nothing to mollify them," says Elizabeth.)

In November 1988, *Sassy* ran yet another sex article. But this one was just as appealing to the magazine's critics as it was to its young, sometimes inexperienced fans. It was titled "Virgins Are Cool."

sex and your body

Sassy's competition lambasted the magazine for its sex coverage. "I don't think that feature is responsible," Robert Brown, associate publisher of *Teen*, has said about the article "Losing Your Virginity." "I think it's offensive."

That depends, of course, on your definition of responsibility. To the *Sassy* staff, it was irresponsible, in light of the threat of AIDS and the possibility of unwanted pregnancy, to pretend that teens weren't having sex; it was irresponsible to talk to teenagers about sex in a way that wouldn't connect with them; it was irresponsible to shy away from subjects that were important to teenagers simply because writing about them might piss off advertisers. Not to mention that it was more irresponsible to pretend that all of its readers were the consummate good girls, that their parents were always right, that sex wasn't the issue that loomed largest in their minds.

In other words, *Sassy*'s definition of responsibility was radically different from *Seventeen*'s. "You weren't like, 'Oh, we've got to give those girls the truth,' " says Crichton, who was in charge of all the articles, of the magazine's traditional role as an extension of the patriarchy. "You were like, 'We've just got to give those girls what's good for them.' "

It's an attitude she probably learned from her boss, Midge Richardson, the editor in chief of *Seventeen* and an ex-nun. Midge grew up in a Catholic family in Los Angeles, a former child star who had appeared in a movie called *The Bachelor and the Bobby-Soxer* with Cary Grant, Myrna Loy, and Shirley Temple. But she put aside her Hollywood life when she found God, joined a convent, and became Sister Agnes, then a Mother Superior. She was heading a high school in her home city when she was stricken with psychosomatic blindness. The doctors told her that she would never regain her sight if she didn't make some major life changes. So she left the convent—and apparently that's all it took—and wrote a memoir about her experience called *The Buried Life*. While she was doing press for the book, an editor at *Glamour* magazine called her up and offered her a job. She accepted.

One day, Alexander Liberman, the legendary Condé Nast editorial director, spotted her in the elevator and asked around about the cute girl who looked like a nun. "She *was* a nun, until recently," he was told. But she was quite fetching without her habit on. In fact, she caught the eye of *Vogue* photographer Gordon Parks, who sent her to France for a $10,000 makeover, including a chic new haircut from Vidal Sassoon. All of which is to say, by the time Jane Pratt appeared on the magazine scene, Midge wasn't totally uncool: she wore Ungaro and Chanel; she dated Burt Reynolds—no rock star, true, but a furry-chested *Cosmo* centerfold all the same; and she later married Hamilton Richardson, a tennis star who had an apartment on Park Avenue, rented a huge house in Southampton, and owned a condo on Palm Beach.

"She was a tough lady. She considered herself always the educator, always tied to young people," says beauty editor Annemarie Iverson. "And that's kind of the way she ran it; it was the mother superior running *Seventeen*." Mary Clarke, who worked at *Seventeen* before getting her job as the beauty editor of *Sassy*, agrees. "She was like a school principal. She would walk down the halls and say, 'Good morning.' " At Monday editorial meetings, she informed the beauty and fashion departments—which consisted of more than a few fair-haired ice queens—what they would cover (she didn't care much about the articles). She would try to fire people because they chewed gum like a cow or didn't know how to bend over properly in their miniskirts.

"It's almost like talking dirty to kids," Richardson said about the *Sassy* sex stories.

But her comments were likely politically motivated. For one thing, the two magazines were at war. (*Sassy*'s 1994 entertainment poll asks, "Who's your favorite dinosaur? T. Rex, Barney, Aerosmith, or Midge Turk Richardson?") For another, despite *Seventeen*'s chaste reputation, some of the stories that ran were as explicit as *Sassy*'s early sex articles. "We actually put in a lot of stuff that people didn't give us any credit for, under the radar," says Crichton. But there were also articles like "How Do I Know if I'm Doing It Right," which was about "performing well" when readers "kiss, hold hands, or express any physical form of affection," and another on sexual dreams. There was even one on—get this—blue balls.

But no one in the press ever mentioned *Seventeen*'s sex articles—even in 1989, when the magazine ran a quiz titled "Are You Ready for Sex?" It sounded suspiciously like *Sassy*'s loss-of-virginity piece, which had gotten its fair share of attention from readers, the religious right, and the competition. In fact, during Crichton's tenure, *Seventeen* increased its coverage of sex, cutting, divorce—the darker side of teenage life—and its circulation increased exponentially. But while its stories increasingly portrayed the real pathologies affecting girls, the tone was always removed and journalistic, which helped the magazine retain its patina of innocence, even among high-school librarians, most of whom shelved the magazine and looked at it closely.

A new magazine with an unexpected voice, *Sassy* was a much more vulnerable target. The religious right wasn't about to go up against the industry's kingpin, which had a pristine reputation among the millions of mothers who happily bought it for their daughters. "*Seventeen*'s dirty little secret is that it's really hard to know whether any of the girls read it. We knew moms read it and filled out subscription cards and renewed it," says David Abrahamson, a professor at Northwestern's Medill School of Journalism. "It wasn't for daughters to enjoy, but for moms to feel good about their daughters possessing."

The companies who ran ads in the publication—and who certainly wanted girls' allowances to line their coffers—kept quiet about the magazine's sexual content as well. "Most people on the advertising side of the business thought of it as a fashion magazine—because that's where the money came from," says Caroline Miller. "But the reality of it is if you talk to girls and you read all the surveys, which we did a lot of, very few people bought it for those fashion stories. They bought it for the personal stuff." Luckily for *Seventeen*, its reputation for covering the lighter side of female adolescence remained an effective cover.

the end of the innocence

While preparing for the June 1989 issue, the *Sassy* staff spent a day going through boxes and boxes of "It Happened to Me"s, looking for submissions about incest. They decided to ring a bell every time they found another one, and that bell rang more than any of them had expected.

The reason for this depressing exercise was that the editorial staff was trying to prove to the business side that an article on incest was imperative. Says Mike, who remembers that there was hesitation, "We were trying to tell them that we're constantly getting letters from girls about having been victims of all this." But not only would an article on incest deal with the most taboo form of sex, it would also tell girls that sometimes their parents are horribly wrong. And undermining the place of parents in their daughters' lives was a tricky undertaking. Still, the staff prevailed, and six months after their last sex article, "Real Stories About Incest" ran. Written by Catherine, it chronicled the tales of three girls who had been through it.

It would prove a Pyrrhic victory, though, as Sandra was asked to step down a month before the piece ran.

"I never decided to sell *Sassy*—I never would have," says Sandra. "Citicorp Venture Capital, who controlled sixty percent of the company, asked me to resign. Clearly they believed someone had to be held accountable for what had happened, and that person was me. It remains the most painful episode of my working career."

"Someone kind of had to take the fall for the boycott," agrees Mary Kaye.

The magazine's buyer, in October 1989, was Lang Communications, owned by Dale Lang. Lang was one of the few small, independent publishers left among the conglomerates. Lang owned a number of feminist-y magazines designed to appeal to the women's movement's growing num-

bers, including *Working Woman*, *Working Mother*, and *Success*. Lang's publications were dedicated to women's newfound fiscal independence: an idea advertisers—eager to be the recipients of women's money, regardless of whether it was earned by them or their husbands—warmed right up to. Advertisers were especially pleased that the magazines weren't particularly political.

Lang himself was dapper and charming, a businessman known as a bit of a swashbuckler, a medium-time player with big dreams, and he was excited by the opportunity to take a flailing publication and turn it around. "I bought *Sassy* because I thought it was a great, great publication. I loved the idea that it was kind of the anti-*Seventeen*," says Lang. He was less attracted to *Sassy*'s sister property. But Citibank, who controlled the sale, wouldn't budge: if Lang wanted *Sassy*, he had to buy *Ms.*, too. "The last thing they wanted to be left with, frankly, was *Ms.* magazine," says Lang. "If somebody was going to have to bury *Ms.* magazine, they were going to take a lot of heat for that—and it wasn't going to be Citibank."

Ms. was an albatross of a business property. "If the editors really gave the readers what they wanted in *Ms.*, the advertisers would run away screaming," says Lang. What they wanted, presumably, were stories like the exclusive the editors scored on the effect the Soviet Union's occupation of Afghanistan had on women. The article generated buzz, but it also made Revlon—a cosmetics company the magazine had pursued for years—jump ship. Why? Revlon was upset that the woman on the cover—a Russian peasant—wasn't wearing any makeup.

That *Ms.* editors refused to bow to the advertisers the magazine relied on for its existence was a constant bone of contention between Steinem and Lang. According to the latter, "I said, 'Gloria, don't you realize that unless the magazine can stop losing money, it can't live? You know? It doesn't have to make money, but it just can't lose money.' "

"Dale Lang was an extremely schlocky guy," counters Steinem. "He was not impossible to work with, because he listened and he wanted to be liked and he wanted to do well. But he had no clue about content at all." (Nor, she says, did he actually understand *Ms.*'s activist mission. "The *Ms.* staff would take off the Martin Luther King, Jr., day as a holiday or go to political rallies in Times Square and the Lang people would say, 'You can't do this because everyone will want to do it.' ")

The two finally came to a kind of truce, agreeing that the magazine couldn't serve both its audience and its advertisers. After ensuring they had enough reader support, they converted the magazine to an ad-free, subscription-only publication.

And in their way, the *Sassy* staff had a similar sense of mission. Initially, the boycott had seemed a bit funny. It had even, to a certain extent, fed the staff's rebellious fantasies, drawing them closer, making them feel more fiercely committed to their work at the magazine. "We were all so young; we kind of didn't give a shit," says Jane. "I remember Christina and I talking about this many times. But we wanted to be thrown out rather than fade away. We much preferred the idea that we had made an impact on teenagers and on the culture in general and that generation,

and that years later people would be talking about *Sassy* and the impact it had—much, much rather that than modify what we were doing, than do something softer and exist for fifty years. We were twenty-five years old—who cares about existing for that long?"

But as the boycott played itself out and *Sassy* lost ad pages and its beloved founder, the situation became less amusing. "It was terrible. We would come in, for years and years and years—we joked, but it was true—we would come in to work not knowing if our desks were still going to be there. We just thought the magazine was going to fold any day," says Jane. "And then we did have to make changes; that was the toughest part of all." *Ms.* may have won editorial freedom under Lang, but *Sassy* did not. The magazine couldn't talk about sex for years.

"It was everyone's first big reality check," says Karen. The staff didn't realize how easy it was for business concerns to trump editorial ones. "We were so spoiled," agrees Christina. "We lived in this little idyllic world where we didn't have to worry about advertising; we were just told to make a magazine that teenagers would respond to. And that's just not the reality of publishing. And once our fairy godmother was gone—once Sandra was gone—it became more real."

When Sandra left, *Sassy* changed. "It was different. It was always stressful in the office," says Cheryl. The editors "did the best they could do, and it was still a good magazine, and readers still loved it. But in some ways, the Moral Majority had done its work."

chapter 4

Celebrity

teenage riot

One day in the summer of 1990, the publicist for the legendary New York noise-rock band Sonic Youth called Christina. To promote their latest album, *Goo*, the band requested press in two publications: *The New York Times Magazine* and *Sassy*. The band had been fans of *Sassy* for a while. "I remember thinking how I wished there was a magazine like *Sassy* when I was a young girl," says bassist Kim Gordon.

Christina told the publicist that Mike wanted to do the interview, but Sonic Youth had other plans. "She called me back and said, 'No, they don't want some guy, they want you,'" remembers Christina.

Sonic Youth has always been known for their innovation in the way they play music. But the real genius of the band has been their ability to spot talent, forging relationships with the coolest artists of the moment: handpicking opening bands like Nirvana, featuring designer Marc Jacobs's clothes in their "Sugar Kane" video, and using artists like Mike Kelley, Gerhard Richter, and Raymond Pettibon for their album art. By seeking out *Sassy*, Sonic Youth not only established the magazine as a vanguard for underground music long before Nirvana broke to mainstream audiences, but enshrined Christina as one of the premier music critics of the early nineties (her taste was so revered that she was once offered a job in A&R for a record label).

"Sonic Youth on $100 a Day," Christina's interview, features her shopping with the band at a downtown flea market. "I remember thinking, 'I'm interviewing Sonic Youth, I have to have really good music-journalist questions, so I look like I know what I'm doing,' " Christina recalls. But as soon as she started asking Kim Gordon how the band got together, Gordon groaned and asked, "Do we have to answer these kinds of questions?" So Christina changed direction and asked her what her favorite color was (it's blue). "Kim was so much happier after that," Christina says. In a nod to the *Tiger Beat* school of teen idolatry, the entire interview is made up of questions about the band's favorite colors (Steve: "green and gray together"), what they were like in high school (Kim: "read Nietszche in class to rebel"), what their least favorite band is (Lee: "Stone Roses and Happy Mondays"), and what they look for in a girl (Thurston: "roundness").

why all the celebrity worship?

Sassy had an ambivalent relationship to celebrity from the very beginning. In the second issue, Karen wrote a story called "Dating a Rock Star." Not only does she make it seem tedious (long hours on a tour bus, band drama), she even makes the sex seem bad. Other reasons to avoid metalheads and troubadours: "There's the smudged mascara (he's always too exhausted to take it off before bed); the bad case of the breakouts (from all that stage makeup); the pale, sickly skin (because he's only really awake when it's dark outside); the flabby, out-of-shape body from too much Howard Johnson food and not enough time to use that new rowing machine on the tour bus." That same issue featured another article by Karen, on a certain redheaded teen pop sensation, called "How Tiffany Ruined My Weekend," wherein she gripes that she spent the day "waiting for a call from a girl whose only New Year's resolution was to grow her own natural fingernails."

In a 1989 ode to Debbie Gibson, Christina notes, in an aside, "I thought she looked good, but then she put on this heinous denim jacket . . . I say this as a friend offering constructive advice." With every issue the magazine seemed to become less self-conscious; soon, Christina was regularly taking on the cultural bread-and-butter of teen magazines, dismissing "Top 40 hell" and huffing that "the creativity of the major networks leaves me breathless." She connected her hatred of individual celebrities to the inanity of the star-making machine: "What is wrong with our society that we elevate sleazoids to celebrity status, take their opinions seriously, *and* make them rich?" she asked.

That sentiment was a part of a June 1992 article, a celebrity snark manifesto of sorts, called

"Why All the Celebrity Worship?" in which Christina spews forth her trademark vitriol about *Beverly Hills, 90210*'s resident hunk Luke Perry (*Sassy* had a deep love-hate relationship with the hugely popular teen drama). "What has [he] done to redeem humanity? At press time, nothing," she writes, then calls her fellow teen mags "mindless pawns in the celeb-making game." She wonders about *Sassy*'s relationship to the entertainment world, since the magazine covered celebrities as much as their competitors did. "Either we are part of the problem, or we are making fun of the whole thing. It depends on how you look at it." That kind of tortured relationship with celebrity became the magazine's signature: celebrating pop culture and hating it at the same time.

Suffice it to say, there was no other teen magazine out there indulging in this kind of postmodern criticism. But Christina's articles could have appeared in another publication that was enjoying its heyday around the same time as *Sassy*: *Spy*. "The New York Monthly" was a hugely influential magazine that was unafraid of the consequences of its celebrity bashing (they once featured a nude photo of pre-Governator Arnold Schwarzenegger next to a picture of his father's Nazi membership card). *Sassy* and *Spy*, along with *The Village Voice*, *Spin*, and *7 Days*, were part of a mini-revolution that was happening in magazines' treatment of celebrities in the late eighties and early nineties. Many young journalists working at these publications had graduated from small liberal-arts colleges where low culture was a subject of scholarly inquiry. And a revolution was happening in pop culture itself: comedian Sandra Bernhard was also deconstructing the celebrity machine in her one-woman show *Without You I'm Nothing*. Even Bernhard's then best friend, Madonna, was analyzing her own fame in her 1991 documentary *Truth or Dare*.

Regardless of outside influence, Christina thinks *Sassy*'s tone was set by the celebrity handlers. "I think I was just annoyed at the way I was being treated by the publicists," she says. Part of her job covering entertainment for *Sassy* was to take handlers' calls. But she also edited the fiction and wrote "What Now" and two or three additional articles a month. So she usually didn't have time to call publicists back. Why bother? If they yelled at her on her answering machine, it made good fodder for the rest of the office to laugh at. Unfortunately for magazine editors, celebrities were outselling models and increasingly becoming standard for magazine covers in the early nineties—which meant that the dreaded publicists gained more and more power. *Sassy* needed to sell at the newsstand, too, and that meant a little more celebrity and publicist ass-kissing was in order. "I was having this visceral, juvenile reaction to it," Christina says. So she decided she wouldn't sugarcoat what stars said or did during interviews, or pretend that everything went well. "And," she shrugs, "nobody stopped me."

So a January 1993 cover line reads: "Shannen Doherty, Pathetic Loser." Christina calls Tori Spelling "Miss Plastic Surgery" in the pages of "What Now." The abrasive Kennedy is called the "most hated MTV VJ" on a cover, and the article itself is simply titled "Deserving of Our Hatred?" *Melrose Place* star Andrew Shue, according to Maureen Callahan, a writer who joined the staff in 1993, "isn't really an apathetic, dim-witted underachiever. He just plays one on TV."

Surprisingly, the most infamous of *Sassy*'s celebrity smackdowns wasn't written by Christina. Mary Ann Marshall, a writer who started in late 1992, penned "Something Does Not Compute," an interview with ditzy Saturday morning TV star Tiffani-Amber Thiessen. Instead of fawning over the brain-dead former beauty queen, *Sassy* refers to her as *"Saved by the Bell*'s Demi-Bimbo"—right on the cover—and makes fun of her when she says she likes "a lot of Shakespeare's lesser-known works . . . like *Hamlet.*" Mary Ann writes, "Oh, I hadn't heard of that one." You can practically see her eyes roll. Reading the article felt like gossiping with your meanest friend. When Tiffani-Amber points out that she was valedictorian of her class of "forty-five, fifty kids," Mary Ann responds—italics her own—"No, she's smarter than *all those people?*"

Tiffani-Amber Thiessen's publicist, Matt Labov, wasn't exactly pleased with the interview. He sent *Sassy* a scathing letter that stated he would

like to go on record with my outrage and disbelief. With any feature interview, talent can be subjected to a fair share of non-positivity, but this "feature" not only crosses that line but plants a flag in the ground proudly saying "negativity." This

kind of press goes far beyond the acceptable motives of keeping readers and advertisers happy; it reveals a hidden agenda of mudslinging and terrorist tactics. It's what we generally expect from tabloids, a category into which this kind of writing puts your magazine, a category we will not work with.

Sassy published his diatribe under the headline "But Shouldn't Bimbodom Be a Crime?"

Labov's ire notwithstanding, the profile was an instant classic with readers. Amy from Hudson, Wyoming, wrote in, "You verified that she is a Marlboro Lights–smoking, complete fake, wannabe, poser, overrated, Brian Austin Green–dating, asinine beast from hell! Oh, yeah, and she obviously has too much air in her head for a brain! Tiffani-Amber, if you're reading this, you're a waste of landmass for a real-life nineties woman."

Instead of feeling disillusioned by hearing the warts-and-all truth about their favorite celebs, *Sassy*'s readers delighted in the magazine's bitchiness, perhaps because Tiffani-Amber's type—the pretty, popular girl who's a little dumb, a little mean, but takes herself very seriously—was instantly recognizable. Mary Ann's unapologetic loathing of her was the wish-fulfillment of anyone who had ever weathered high school. *Sassy*'s trademark cranky celebrity coverage rang true; Jessica Nordell, in a open letter to Jane Pratt in the Harvard *Crimson*, writes that part of the joy of *Sassy* "was that it applauded the idea that movie stars are little more than pretty faces and talking heads, and that real people doing real things were a lot more worthy of our attention. Isn't the fact that we get excited when a star says something coherent an example of the exception that proves the rule?"

On the other hand, Jane says, "We were very excited about the people who were worth being excited about. When Christina would fly off to interview Johnny Depp, we would literally be jumping up and down." Jane was also particularly excited about R.E.M., and made constant reference to her friendship with the band. (They were such good friends that singer Michael Stipe felt it necessary to tell her that he didn't think *Sassy* was such a great name for a teen magazine "because it had the word *ass* in it and if you change the first two letters it says *pussy*.") When singer Stipe would telephone during a staff meeting, Jane would always take the call. "I remember us all sitting on the floor. She's sitting at her desk and would turn around and be like, 'Hiiiii' and curl up," says Jessica Vitkus, who started working at *Sassy* in 1989. Later Jane gushed in her "Diary" column about appearing in the band's video for "Shiny Happy People."

Perhaps the best example of this symbiotic relationship appeared in the December 1989 issue, where all copies of *Sassy* included a flexidisc—a very thin, bendable plastic record—of R.E.M. covering Syd Barrett's "Dark Globe." "We had wanted to do a flexidisc for a long time. Because I was friends with R.E.M., I just asked them if they would give us one," says Jane. Paying for

the rights to the song would have cost about $25,000—way over the budget of cash-strapped Lang Communications—so the band covered the expense as a favor to Jane. The record became an instant collector's item. On the day the issue came out, Jane was walking by Tower Records on Fourth Street and saw that they had sold almost every copy of the issue. She was elated—until she saw a trashcan full of *Sassy*s right outside. Fans of the band—but not the magazine—had torn out the flexidisc and ditched the publication.

Sassy fans loved it, too, though. "We were introducing R.E.M. to the younger generation. At the time that *Sassy* came out, their audience was more college-age," says Jane. "We were bringing in the new kids on the block—the teen girls."

Beyond bringing more fans to celebrities who didn't necessarily target teens, *Sassy* could also help change the images of more mainstream stars. Actress Mayim Bialik was first discovered playing the kid version of Bette Midler in the weeper *Beaches* and went on to star in the sitcom *Blossom*, where she was seen as just another cute kid actress. She was a longtime *Sassy* fan and was thrilled to meet Christina, who saw something more in her. She loved Bialik's quirky thrift-shop style and atypical Hollywood looks; *Sassy* went on to feature her on the cover of their November 1992 issue.

Bialik had appeared in plenty of other magazines, which always had the same attitude: that celebrities could do or say no wrong. "They would write that you're the sweetest person on the planet no matter what," she says. The staff at

Sassy, she says, "interpreted people as they were and not as their teen audience would want to see them." In other words, *Sassy* was discriminating. "We wouldn't just profile somebody because they had a popular movie out," says Mike. "It had to be somebody we liked and respected."

It felt like the bond between celebrities and *Sassy* was real, not orchestrated. In the article "How *Sassy* Changed My Life" in the March 1993 fifth-anniversary issue, various stars gush about the magazine. Courtney Love says, "When I first saw *Sassy*, I got really jealous of teenage girls 'cause all I had was yucky *Teen* magazine and white, white, white *Seventeen* magazine. If I had *Sassy* as a teen I'm sure I would have turned out with a stronger moral fiber, but I probably wouldn't have started a band. If I had *Sassy*, I would probably be teaching retarded children." Mayim Bialik, bands Ween and Sonic Youth, MTV VJ Tabitha Soren, Bratmobile's Erin Smith, designers Todd Oldham and Anna Sui, and director John Waters offered similarly heartfelt rhapsodies.

indie invasion

And speaking of Courtney Love, she and Kurt Cobain—rock's most infamous couple—appeared on the cover of *Sassy* in April 1992. It was Kurt and Courtney's (or "Kurtney," as Christina called them in the pages of "What Now," heralding the era of Bennifer, Brangelina, and TomKat) first magazine appearance together and, given that they'd had offers from every major music maga-

zine, a real coup for *Sassy*. Love's publicist at Hole's then label, Caroline, was a friend of Christina's, and she made the article happen. "We got in there just before everyone else wanted to," Christina remembers.

Strangely, Nirvana's circle was less than six degrees of separation from *Sassy*'s: in an early issue, *Sassy* had included a short blurb on a new deodorant called Teen Spirit. They gave the product a rave review (the ad for it was, after all, on the facing page) but said "gag on the name." Kathleen Hanna of Bikini Kill was rumored to have read the piece and spray-painted SMELLS LIKE TEEN SPIRIT on Kurt's wall. "Smells Like Teen Spirit" became the name of Nirvana's first single from *Nevermind*, the Seattle-based indie trio's major label debut. It climbed to the top of the Billboard charts, beginning the popular phase of the grunge era.

A Nirvana fan since their days on Sub Pop, Christine Muhlke was Christina's intern at the time. When she heard that Christina was going to interview Kurt and Courtney, Christine begged her to be allowed to come along. The band was in New York to tape an episode of *Saturday Night Live*. Kurt and Courtney were so late to the interview that there was some question of whether the couple would even show up; when they finally arrived, they both seemed to be on something. Either way, it was a memorable interview. "Courtney was so fantastic, talking about how Kurt liked her and didn't like skinny models," says Christine. She adds that "Kurt barely got to speak, but when he spoke, he was so beautiful and articulate and lovely, and we just kind of sat there and we were so overwhelmed by these really powerful, truly punk people." She said half the fun was watching Christina interact with the hyperactive Courtney. "I think she was intimidated," says Christine. Christina may have been a New York scenester, but Courtney Love was like Nancy Spungen come back to life.

The interview was a high point in the annals of both indie rock and *Sassy*. Kurt would eventually succumb to a drug-addled depression; a documentary would accuse Courtney of murdering her more-famous husband; their daughter, Frances Bean, would be forcibly removed from Courtney's home; and, years later, Courtney would be dragged out of her Manhattan apartment wailing about a botched abortion. But that spring, the couple was on the verge of making major pop-culture history, and they were very much in love. In a now famous moment in the much-reprinted interview, Courtney apologizes to Christina for a blemish on her face: "Sorry about this zit," she says. "Zits are beauty marks," an enraptured Kurt replies. "It's poignant for me to think about even now," one twentysomething told *Sassy* fan Rebecca L. Fox in "*Sassy* All Over Again." Fox opines, "As another reader whom *Sassy* assured could be loved, zits and all, I know exactly how she feels."

Years before Kurt and Courtney became household names and helped usher alternative culture into the mainstream, *Sassy* supported independent music. Christina launched "Cute Band Alert"—the title was a parody of teen-magazine speak—in "What Now" (once described in *Sassy* as "the monthly column of what Christina likes, who Christina thinks is cute, what outrages Christina, people Christina hates, and people Christina *really* hates") in February 1990. "It was supposed to be a one-off," Christina remembers. She got a black-and-white glossy of the band Bullet LaVolta in the mail and thought they were cute. There were so many write-in requests for a follow-up that in January 1991 the section became a regular column in "What Now." Publicists and band members alike started lobbying Christina to be featured. "All these cool bands wanted to be in it," she says. In fact, the alumni list of "Cute Band Alert" reads like an encyclopedia entry for nineties alternative music: Bikini Kill, Blonde Redhead, Chavez, Heavenly, Sloan, Ween, and That dog. It is also the place that massively successful and notorious indie bands like Guided by Voices, Jon Spencer Blues Explosion, and Superchunk got their first piece of teen press.

Sassy was one of the first nonmusic magazines to cover underground music. "In the eighties, there was an us-versus-them situation: us being the underground and them being mainstream American culture. They just never met. They were in two parallel universes," says K Records founder and "What Now" regular Calvin Johnson. "The mainstream press mostly saw indie labels as vanity publishing, as if the band was not on a 'real' record label because no one else would put it out. The fact that Christina accepted us at face value was startling."

Sassy's love affair with all things indie (not

just indie rock, but indie actors, directors, and comic-book artists were featured in its pages) was, according to Christina, entirely organic. "What I was writing about evolved with what I was interested in. Through people I met in my job, I got exposed to all these different things," she says. "It was like a privilege to be there because people thought *Sassy* was cool, so they'd gravitate toward us." In turn, the punk-rock and indie world got a frisson of excitement seeing themselves in a magazine you could find on grocery-store shelves. "The funniest thing about *Sassy*'s coverage was that it was so inside," says music critic Ann Powers. "Here was something that should have been the organ of mainstream pop culture, taking the indie-rock stance."

There was, of course, the inevitable backlash from older veterans of the music scene, who frowned upon appearing alongside reviews of bland mainstream pop acts like Samantha Fox (even though Mike thought her album merited less than a star). Teen girls' taste was so derided that no "serious" musical act courted their devotion. "A lot of punks picked on *Sassy* for bringing bands like Blonde Redhead to the forefront," says fan Annie Tomlin (who was such a *Sassy* devotee growing up that she and her friends would stage mock photo shoots based on layouts they saw in the magazine). But Tomlin feels that Christina's coverage of indie music was an important lifeline for teens like her. "For girls who grew up in the proverbial middle of nowhere, it was our big connection to something different. It planted a cultural seed that wound up making me interested

in different cultures that I couldn't have discovered without the magazine." Constance Hwong remembers that, pre-*Sassy*, "I thought *indie* meant 'from India.' I started listening to Sonic Youth, 7 Year Bitch, Liz Phair, and probably a bunch of other things, all because of *Sassy* and their music reviews."

Covering bands geared to the college crowd gave the magazine indie cred—something previously unheard of in the teen market. Because let's face it: *Seventeen* and company had never been particularly hip—or even discerning—in their celebrity coverage. Of course, in *Seventeen* there was the occasional nod to the token alternative act that had found mainstream success, like the Cure or R.E.M. Sarah Crichton remembers pushing for a Beastie Boys story in the late 1980s. This was when the group had naked girls dancing in bamboo cages onstage—before they found Tibetan Buddhism and started dating feminists. The shoot was all set when Crichton's phone rang: "Midge was calling from a plane, and she told me that the Beastie Boys were performing with a giant penis onstage, and she said, 'Cancel that shoot!' " She pauses, "Well, the Beastie Boys did not appear in *Seventeen*."

By 1990, *Seventeen* was noticing *Sassy*'s emphasis on alternative culture and taking baby steps toward upping its cool quotient. On the one hand, it would feature an obscure indie band no one had ever really heard of, like the Lilac Time, but then it would also run a story on Swedish metal-lite band Roxette. By 1992, it would feature a big photo and review of gray-haired Leonard

Cohen (an odd pick for a teen magazine) alongside a write-up of British shoegaze band Slowdive and compare their ethereal music to—*shudder*—Wilson Phillips. That same year, they pushed the feminist girl-rock envelope with the article "Babes in Boyland," where they asked "the coolest women in rock" (including Kim Gordon) what it's really like "when you're the only gal in the band." By the early nineties, *Seventeen* had gotten the memo that times were changing, and they tried to reflect that in their celebrity and music coverage, but they lacked the inner compass of cool—namely, Christina Kelly—that *Sassy* had.

It took a certain amount of conviction on *Sassy*'s part to put underground celebrities in its pages, but once they did, even the magazine's business side embraced alternative culture. *Sassy* frequently featured a half-page Social Distortion ad next to one hawking tampons. Companies who had previously advertised only in *Spin* and *Rolling Stone* soon began to purchase ad space in *Sassy*.

Sassy's recurring coverage of Sonic Youth (sharing their fish-taco recipe; Kim Gordon getting her hair done with the staff), the Beastie Boys (baking a birthday cake for the magazine), Matador Records (the label of various "Cute Band Alerts"), and various other key figures in the nineties indie explosion made it seem like there was an alternative mafia represented in *Sassy*.

The column "Dear Boy," where readers sent in their relationship questions for a famous guy to answer, was launched in June 1993. The column allowed *Sassy* to give yet more face time to indie-rock hotshots like Beck, Mike D. (of the Beastie Boys), Billy Corgan (of Smashing Pumpkins), and Iggy Pop. The questions were typical teen territory—"There's this guy that I really like. He tells everyone that he doesn't even like me as a friend, but when we're alone together we do things that are reserved for people who think of each other as more than friends. What do I do?"—but the rock stars got to show a softer side. Thurston Moore from Sonic Youth replied to the aforementioned question, saying, "The guy's a jerk. I know that won't discourage you from liking him, but he's got a major personality flaw: disrespecting you. Next time you're alone with him and he tries to get 'friendly,' tell him your friend Thurston Moore wants to kick his ass. And then tell him why."

the *sassy* celebrity launch pad

The *Sassy* editors were able to pinpoint some ineffable quality in two other celebrities who would go on to become avatars of Generation X. The first is Chloë Sevigny. "Chloë was walking by on the street and Andrea just kind of grabbed her," says Mary. Chloë became an intern at the magazine and modeled in a number of their shoots. She was there at the same time as Christine Muhlke, who says, "She wore really big hats that she made, and she had really big pants, and I just had a horrible, horrible girl crush on her." This was, of course, before Jay McInerney catapulted her to It Girl status when he wrote about her in *The New Yorker*. Since Andrea launched her

career, Chloë has become a major pop-culture fig-
ure, starring in Larry Clark's *Kids*, garnering an
Oscar nomination for her role in *Boys Don't Cry*,
regularly appearing in fashion magazines like
Vogue and *Harper's Bazaar* and in ad campaigns
for favorite hipster brands like Miu Miu and
M.A.C., and strutting naked down a catwalk in
Sonic Youth's "Sugar Kane" video. (She met the
band through *Sassy* after former intern Daisy Von
Furth recommended her for the part.)

It was Christina who made initial contact with
Spike Jonze, another of the magazine's favorite
subjects, before he secured his import in late-
twentieth-century culture by directing Beastie
Boys videos and Oscar-nominated films *Adapta-
tion* and *Being John Malkovich*. Charles Aaron, a
former "staff boy" (a notoriously ambiguous
gofer-type position), remembers spotting Spike in
the *Sassy* office. "He's sitting on the floor, next to
Christina's desk, going through zines and making weird jokes."

Spike's relationship with *Sassy* happened entirely by accident. He was living in Los Angeles
and working with friends Andy Jenkins and Mark
"Lew" Lewman on *Homeboy*, a magazine that began in 1986 and that combined skateboarding
and bike riders alongside comic-book creators,
musicians, artists, and, as they put it, "weirdos
and bums."

One *Homeboy* reader felt dissed by the magazine and, as retaliation, sent out "bill me later"
blow-in subscription cards with *Homeboy*'s address to a random array of magazines, including
Pig Farmer, *Guns & Ammo*, *Coal Miner Monthly*,

and *Sassy*. Out of curiosity, the editors flipped
through the magazines; somehow, *Sassy* stuck.
(Not least because despite their never having paid
for the subscription, *Sassy* kept arriving each
month.) "Nobody wanted to admit to reading it,
but we all poked through it," says Lew. Spike
would occasionally read aloud from *Sassy* while
they were driving to shoots. They had a certain
fascination with the female *Sassy* reader. "We
were eighteen or nineteen, and it was a window
into how girls thought and felt," Spike says.

After reading *Sassy* for a while, Lew decided
that he was going to make contact with the magazine. He randomly picked Christina Kelly's name
off the masthead of *Sassy* and mailed her an eclectic collection of his desk detritus. Charmed,
she wrote him back, and the two started a mail
correspondence. Finally, a series of hangouts between the *Homeboy* boys and the *Sassy* girls was
arranged.

Lew first met Jane and Christina, who were in
Palm Springs for a Miss Teen USA competition (for what would become Christina's article
"Beauty Pageants Are a Lot Like the Army" in
February 1990). A few months later, Lew, Andy,
and Spike went to a bike event in New York and
stopped by the *Sassy* offices. "It felt a little like
meeting our East Coast counterparts," Spike remembers. Even though the *Sassy* staff was for the
most part only a few years older than the *Homeboy* boys, they seemed "like sophisticated New
Yorkers," he says. The guys were particularly impressed that they could spot rapper Special Ed
and prank call Christina's friends from the office.

The three became fixtures in the office and minor celebrities in the magazine, with Lew penning several articles for *Sassy*. (In fact, Lew and Christina dated briefly.) Spike frequently appeared in "What Now," sometimes to his chagrin. Christina and Lew decided it would be funny to have a "Win a Date with Spike Jonze" contest one month. "They didn't tell me about it until I saw it in the magazine," says Spike. "I was so embarrassed and humiliated and mad."

Meanwhile, *Homeboy* was on its last legs. It was one of the few publications out there that targeted adolescent to postadolescent guys. But with a circulation of just fifty thousand, it was basically a glorified zine.

On the heels of *Homeboy*'s decline, Lew, Spike, and Andy had an idea for another kind of magazine for guys. The three created a mock table of contents and article layout, and Jane set up a meeting with Dale Lang, who listened to their pitch. But Lang thought he had too much on his own publishing agenda to do it. He suggested that they put out a first issue by themselves and see how it went. Dejected and lacking the funds to self-publish, they were about to consider other employment. Then they got a call from Lang, about two weeks later, asking if they still wanted to do a magazine. Lang had recently been asked by a journalist at *The Wall Street Journal* why there weren't any male publications in the same vein as *Sassy*. (*Details* had just gone from a local New York publication to a national magazine, but it skewed affluent and effete. The only other general-interest magazine for boys was *Boys' Life*,

and you had to be a Boy Scout to receive it.) Lang claimed to already have a title in the works. He set the guys up in the Lang Communications West Coast ad-sales office, in a fancy suite on the twenty-fourth floor of a building on Wilshire Boulevard.

The first of issue of *Dirt* came out in September 1991 and was polybagged with *Sassy*. The cover featured a burning TV set (it was real, not Photoshopped) and the words "Youth Culture?" with smaller photos of such early nineties icons as MTV vixen Kari Wuhrer, rapper Ice T, and a snowboarder. Lew was the editor, Spike was the photographer, and Andy was the art director. "The magazine world has fallen short of producing anything for, ahem, young men, with a general interest in life itself," Lew writes in his first editor's letter. "And a whole lot of subjects fall into the category of daily living, so that's basically what you can expect to find within *Dirt*. Sports, music, art, chicks, cars, celebrities, style, girls, motorcycles, females, global issues, current events, women, junk food, video games, and stone cold babes." It was a mere fifty-two pages in length but was chock full of everything they promised: a column called "Junk Drawer" that served as *Dirt*'s answer to "What Now," a story on the life of a gangster, Q&As with Ian MacKaye of Fugazi and the supercross racer Jeff Stanton, and the very *Sassy*-esque "Idiot's Guide to First Dates." There was a guys-only survey enclosed to test readers' reactions. They got seventeen thousand responses in ten days.

In a magazine world where demographics—

not psychographics—still ruled, the fact that the magazine was so varied in terms of content made it hard to pinpoint. At *Homeboy*, the reader was clearly defined as someone who skated or rode BMX. "We couldn't say that about the *Dirt* reader," says Andy. "We liked to think our reader was a like-minded fellow who dug the content we filled the magazine with." Being in the same publishing house as *Sassy* was an important connection, but all the other magazines at Lang were geared toward women, so *Dirt*'s articles on crazy bike messengers and rebel soapbox derbies were maybe, as Andy posits, packed with "a little too much testosterone" for the average *Sassy* reader.

But for all the boy energy in *Dirt*, they certainly weren't chauvinists. "We didn't want to do cheesecake photos of girls," Lew explains, "but we never fully grasped how to deal with sexuality in there." They had a chorus of girl voices in the form of the *Sassy* staff, who often wrote for *Dirt* (just as Lew wrote for *Sassy*). They offered relationship advice, as in the feminist-tinged article "Maybe This Is Why You Can't Get a Girlfriend" or their column "Dear Girl," in which Drew Barrymore, Kim Gordon, and Laura Ballance from Superchunk would dish out girl advice to readers.

For *Dirt*'s small size and irregular publication (it came out more or less seasonally), it managed to get a lot of fans—both *Sassy* readers and celebrities. Kim Gordon jokingly told the editors that Sonic Youth's album *Dirty* was named in honor of the magazine. Fugazi, a band notoriously elusive to the mainstream press, granted *Dirt* an interview. Director John Waters sent them

a postcard saying how much he loved *Dirt*. They got writers like Hugh Gallagher and Douglas Coupland to contribute, and Sofia Coppola and the Beastie Boys were frequently spotted in their pages. Lew once sent a bunch of issues of *Dirt* to Cameron Crowe, who directed *Say Anything*, *Singles*, and *Almost Famous*, and who had been his favorite writer since high school, with a note saying, "I wish you were my friend." Crowe sent him back a note that read, "Mark, I am your friend." Lew remembers, "That got me so high."

Despite *Dirt*'s buzz, however, there was still pressure from New York to add fashion and grooming to the magazine to aid in getting ad dollars from big-money cosmetics companies. "In my eyes it just seemed to undermine the content," Andy says. The three guys normally got their clothes from the Goodwill, or for free from skate companies. Having to use models dressed in mall clothes, they feared, would "pull away from any credibility we might have had. I think we made it work for a while, but it got harder as time went on—harder to be clever about it when we were being sent the goofiest shit to put people in. And the irony is that it didn't pull in any advertising."

From an ad-sales standpoint, *Dirt* was a hard sell because there was no precedent, and no discernible competition for the magazine. Dale Lang came up with alternative ways to market it, making a deal with Marvel Comics to polybag various comic books with *Dirt* and sell them in comic shops. But since the average comic-book reader fell off at about fifteen years old, and the average

Dirt reader began at about fifteen, it wasn't the best fit. "I don't feel anyone at Lang understood what we wanted to do and how we wanted to do it," Andy says (except for the *Sassy* staff, of course). Ultimately, the *Dirt* staff felt misunderstood, like they were three kids from L.A. in flannel shirts and jeans with funny ideas. Andy says, "The way we handled things was seen as unorthodox in the world of Lang, and so we never jived or meshed."

After about a year of producing *Dirt*, the three went on a creative retreat, which consisted of them driving around L.A., going to the Holiday Inn in Torrance, and staying up late trying to come up with a big-picture plan. They decided that they had been trying too hard to please the publisher and to make the magazine broadly general interest when their own interests were more niche. "We decided we should stop doing it," Spike remembers, "or do it in a way that's inspired." So for issue six they took a more conceptual approach and did a tour issue, driving across the country for an entire month, hanging out with friends like the Breeders in Ohio, or meeting up with folksinger R. A. Williams.

The deal with Marvel Comics was clearly not working, but ESPN was launching its younger-skewing brother network, ESPN2, and became an investor in the magazine. By that time Andy wanted out and Spike had already begun directing music videos (for the likes of the Beastie Boys, whom he had met through *Dirt*), so Lew was carrying the magazine on his own. But everything came together for their last issue, called "People, Places, and Things That Made Us Who We Are." It included an essay by Hugh Gallagher about the deaths of River Phoenix and Kurt Cobain. The guys thought it was the best issue yet, the realization of their initial intention. But, according to Spike, "Dale Lang was freaked out. He thought it was too dark and too weird." It was never printed, and *Dirt* folded in 1995.

Lew, Spike, and Andy's work with *Dirt* and *Sassy* gave them a public forum where they could experiment with their burgeoning creative impulses. Andy went on to become the creative director for the hugely popular skate labels Girl and Chocolate, and Lew dabbled in advertising, wrote, and spent a few years in Costa Rica.

As for Spike, Chloë, and countless other up-and-coming actors, future cultural creators, and underground legends: "I still remember all these people when they were teenagers, and have now become sort of larger-than-life and have managed to turn themselves into these kinds of iconic characters," says Charles Aaron. "*Sassy* was the place where they entered the world. It seems like a welcoming way to come into the spotlight."

chapter 5

Girl Culture

girls, girls, girls

Dolls. Dress-up. Slumber parties. Make-overs. First kisses. Saturdays spent at the mall. Gum-chewing. Boy bands. Teen magazines had always covered these aspects of female life with the utmost earnestness. The male mainstream had deemed all these things silly. Second Wave feminists, in their attempt to be seen as equals, had denigrated it all as fluff served up to distract an impressionable population from weightier issues.

Sassy unapologetically celebrated the pop-cultural ephemera of girls' lives. In the magazine's philosophy, being a girl—and all the mass-market accoutrements that helped define girlhood—was good. This ethic was the original premise of what is now known as "girl culture," the formation of which began with a feminist impulse to reclaim the undervalued artifacts of girlhood as a means of reminding girls of a time when they were powerful and strong.

If it sounds counterintuitive—that an eleven-year-old sporting jelly bracelets up to her elbows and dancing around her room to "Like a Virgin" had any kind of larger import—consider "Why You Liked

Yourself Better When You Were 11," an article that appeared in *Sassy*'s July 1991 issue. In it, the magazine documents the findings of Dr. Carol Gilligan, a Harvard psychologist (and latter-day girl-culture icon) whose ideas on young women's self-esteem are espoused in her seminal work, *In a Different Voice*. *Sassy* paraphrased: "When girls are little, they are true to their beliefs. They speak their minds. If they're angry, they let you know. When someone asks them a question, they answer it with confidence. If they don't agree with what they're told to do, they disobey. Pre-teenage girls are proud of being different, and they know that resisting authority is okay." But according to Gilligan, women go through a crisis of confidence at puberty, their self-esteem plummets, and they never truly recover. Gilligan posits that this is because America views boys as the norm: girls are different, and their way of being in the world isn't validated. To validate them, to tell girls that who they are and what they are interested in is good, is an intrinsically feminist act.

Sassy recognized the power of pop culture to create girls' sense of self, but unlike the unsympathetic mass media and the disapproving Second Wave feminists, they didn't denigrate it. Instead, the magazine assumed that girls were talking back to the TV, active participants in their cultural interactions, able to call pop culture on its flaws without having to write it off altogether. Thus, Christina could enjoy "Under the Bridge" while railing against Red Hot Chili Peppers' sexist antics. "Girls like my friends and me, who were

drawn to the TV shows and fashion aimed at our generation, were encouraged to look at it with a critical eye, but not discouraged from our interest in it," says fan Anastasia Cole Plakias. When *Sassy* published its cast of *90210* paper dolls in September 1991, it was so girls could enjoy them on two levels: there was the sheer nostalgic joy in cutting out popular teen soap characters and dressing them up, and the simultaneous self-mocking that you would ever do such a thing. The glee in doing it was ironically cool. This meta-appreciation was simply nonexistent in the excruciatingly earnest world of teen magazines.

Journalists like those on the *Sassy* staff, who were influenced by academia, were "all about the importance of popular culture," says Ann Powers. "There was a sense that it could change your life, a sense of urgency about it. There was potential for popular culture to elevate your identity, especially for girls." So *Sassy* used the word *girl* knowingly, liberally, and lovingly. Mary and Andrea got giddy over the idea of clipping plastic barrettes in their hair or wearing baby-doll dresses and tiaras to the prom. And unlike *Seventeen*, *YM*, and *Teen*, which gave readers advice on how to erase all traces of indelicate, ultrafeminine personality traits, *Sassy* ran articles like "Your Guide to the Perfect Crying Fit," which dared to pose the question "Why shouldn't girls cry as loud and often as they please?" and ran a back-page column called "Working Our Nerves," which each month highlighted a new object of the staff's derision, from the patriarchy (with an image of a presidential cabinet used to illustrate the concept), to misplaced quotation marks, to Jacinta's public displays of affection with her boyfriend, Andy (whom she ended up marrying).

It made sense in an era defined by identity politics—in which groups of people used their status as members of marginalized groups to push for change—to rally around girlhood. Over the years, *Sassy* ran disparate articles about boys, fashion, beauty, food, and culture that, taken separately, aren't easily distinguishable from what *Seventeen*, *YM*, and *Teen* were covering. But collectively, they were part of a larger mandate to celebrate girls and their culture, proving to a population as diverse as American teenage girls that they share experiences all their own.

The magazine was "really good at capturing a *real* girl culture, meaning that it wasn't all about dieting and three-hundred-dollar moisturizers and model stuff that only one percent of the population knew about or could identify with," says fan Millie di Chirico.

Since the beginning, the magazine had told real girls' first-person tales in its "It Happened to Me" column (*Seventeen* had long run a similar column), but the magazine also made a point of showing real girls—not models—in regular sections like "On the Road." Part of the reason for the magazine's yearly Sassiest Girl in America contest was, according to Karen, to tell readers that "we don't want to do a model search. We want to do something deeper and richer than that, that acknowledges that we're not just look-

ing for the skinny girl from L.A." Girls won points for being cool, offbeat, socially active, and politically conscious.

When Caroline Miller came to *Seventeen* in 1994, she used her signature column, "School Zone," to showcase tribes of real teens in high schools across the country—but they were well-lit, poreless, and glamorized.

the beauty myth demystified

By the late eighties, when *Sassy* launched, women and teenage girls had already endured half a decade of fitness fanaticism, an anti-feminist backlash that insisted that only through endless workouts and restrictive eating habits could a girl simultaneously prove that she was like a man (rigorous, disciplined, deserving of a climb up the corporate ladder instead of being waylaid on the mommy track) *and* worthy of male attention. From Jane Fonda's workout tapes to Linda Hamilton's supertoned physique in 1991's *Terminator 2*, the cult of the body reached its apotheosis. Though a new emphasis on exercise may have been good for certain sports-inclined women, an athletic body felt like yet another ideal that many women couldn't live up to. Talk about an effective way of making sure women wouldn't become too smart, too academic, too big for their britches! After all, who had time to concentrate on schoolwork when it took nearly every ounce of a girl's mental and physical energy to stick with this dogmatic regimen? Diet stories were a *Seven-*

teen staple; often a reader would find more than one in an issue, with subtitles like "How Not to Eat Your Way Through College" or warnings that "extra pounds can keep a girl from joining in, speaking up, reaching out."

But *Sassy* didn't fall prey to idealizing appearance obsession. From the beginning, Jane refused to run the ubiquitous dieting stories that littered other teen magazines and fed into the ongoing epidemic of eating disorders and unhealthy body preoccupations. Instead, *Sassy* ran articles like "13 Reasons Not to Diet" (one of the reasons, of course, was that it would impair your cognitive abilities). And though it ran the de rigueur workout article, *Sassy* gave it a decidedly feminist spin by stating, "It's not about exercising to get smaller, it's about exercising to get stronger." Remember: this was a decade before *Buffy*.

Of course, the ads that accompanied the magazine editorial often undermined the editors' mission to downplay the importance of popularity and conventional beauty. *Sassy* could only compete by taking whatever ads came its way, and that included such female-unfriendly plugs as the Clairol shampoo ad that showed a smug supermodel-type alongside copy reading, "The body? Maybe. But the hair can be yours." And while *Sassy* had to provide complementary copy for its biggest advertisers, it also rebelled whenever possible. For example, like the other magazines in its category, *Sassy* often ran ads for products that promised to give insecure teenage girls bigger breasts and thinner thighs; but it also ran an article titled "Karen Tries to Get Thinner Thighs . . . Through the Mail" that debunked the utility of any of said products—not to mention the antifeminist, female-body-hating impetus behind them.

Sassy was masterful at finding the kernel of feminism in places where others didn't bother to look, even though it was right in front of them, and that includes the twin nadirs of *Ms.* magazine: fashion and beauty. *Ms.*, once it went ad-free, had the luxury of refusing to push product, but a consumer magazine like *Sassy* was the perfect place to merge fashion and feminism. The women's movement was one of the most anticapitalist movements in American history, and though the *Sassy* staffers were staunchly feminist, a teen magazine could stay alive only by running fashion and beauty ads and, hence, fashion and beauty stories. But *Sassy* made the situation work in tandem with their engaging new brand of feminism. (And sometimes the stories were slyly political: one thumbed its nose at its beauty advertisers, with their high-priced products, by telling girls how to make their own. How 'bout dying your hair with Jell-O instead of spending eight dollars on a box of Clairol?)

Sassy was deconstructing images of beauty even before the 1991 publication of Naomi Wolf's groundbreaking book *The Beauty Myth: How Images of Beauty Are Used Against Women*, which argued that women could never be equal to men so long as they were tyrannized by unnatural, unachievable images. "How We Make This Girl Gorgeous (and other tricks magazines use to get teeth whiter, hips slimmer and breasts bigger)" was a lesson in media literacy, showing girls the way companies tricked them into wanting to look like women who didn't exist in nature. Similarly, "Why Your Breasts Aren't as Weird as You Think" called beauty standards themselves into question.

"We were very aware—with fashion and beauty texts in particular—of never, ever making the person who is reading them hate themselves," says Karen, who, in the beginning, wrote most of them. So a bathing suit story features a bikini for girls with a "cute little round tummy" and a one-piece for a "bodacious butt." The story didn't presume girls felt like they had figure flaws—they just recast the flaws and told girls how to deal with them. Karen says, "We also didn't want to do 'Oh, you're perfect, you're fine.' Nobody believes that bullshit. But there had to be a middle ground between 'Go shoot yourself' and platitudes."

When Amber Drea discovered *Sassy* she was "happy to make it my number one magazine and get rid of all my *YM*s, which just made me feel gross—like I didn't stand a chance at being pretty, ever."

Instead of humiliating girls into eating their broccoli, *Sassy* celebrated the way real teenagers eat. Hence, one of the most remembered stories of all time: "Our First Annual Junk Food Taste Off." "We convened a panel of convenience-store connoisseurs: Margie Ingall, Mike, Mary Ann, Kim France, and Andrea T. For four diarrhea-

inducing days we tasted sixty-four junky treats," the article opens. After an explanation of the categories and how each junk food will be rated, the staff tries the pork rinds:

MARGIE: As a Jew, I am flatly refusing to taste the pork rinds.

KIM: As a Jew, I am pleased to sample the pork rinds.

MARY ANN: As a human being, I am not going to sample them.

MARGIE: You must. You have no religious grounds.

KIM: They are quite delightful. Big and light like popcorn, then they crunch down to something small and nice.

ANDREA: The texture of sunburned skin.

MARY ANN: These are repulsive beyond explanation. Words fail me.

MIKE: I like the idea of, like, meat being integrated into a salty, fried, crispy thing . . . It's good.

On plantain chips:

MARGIE: Look, there's a little lesson about "What is a plantain" on the back.

ANDREA: The PBS of junk food.

On plain M & M's:

ANDREA: What does green mean again?

KIM: It doesn't mean *that* unless it's peanut.

MARGIE: I heard it meant that.

"That junk-food survey ought to go down in journalistic history," says Elisa Ung. "I remember sitting outside and reading that and laughing so hard my stomach hurt. Constance Hwong agrees. "I remember laughing out loud when reading it. It sounds like something me and my friends would do."

But despite their progressive stance, the *Sassy* staff was certainly not unanimous in its pursuit of alternative beauty ideals. The images in the magazine were hardly fat-positive, especially as heroin-chic waifs like Kate Moss came into vogue in the early nineties. "There was always a fight with the editors from the beauty and fashion department because they still went for the anorexic models and we always wanted to use more real people," says Mary Kaye of the features department. *Sassy*'s models may have been less homogenous compared to its competition—black girls with Afros; white girls with sad faces and long, stringy hair or super-short bleached hair; girls with body piercings—but they were never, ever heavy.

Sassy redefined the very purpose of fashion and beauty products and rituals in girls' lives. According to the magazine, you could use your appearance to assert your (unconventional) identity—"Read this before you RSVP or risk being one of the crowd" trumpeted a "Very Party" fashion story that simultaneously mocked and championed conformity. Or you could use it to embody your (left-wing, feminist) politics—as evidenced in a fashion shoot that featured leather-free shoes even a vegan could love. In *Sassy*, the

female body could be an instrument of liberation.

Sassy's fashion coverage would infuse the tenor of girl culture for years to come. After all, young feminists never really identified with their mothers' bra-burning—but they needed something to wear to all those protests and poetry slams. These Third Wavers owe a serious debt of gratitude to Andrea, who in 1993 professed her love of baby tees in the magazine's pages. Higher-ups at Urban Outfitters took notice of the trend and began producing shrunken, belly-baring tees for adults—the same T-shirts the girls at April 2004's March for Women's Lives were wearing, bearing slogans like THIS IS WHAT A FEMINIST LOOKS LIKE. From a glitter-girl story to grunge prom (pair Doc Martens with baby-doll dresses, why don't you?) to "Our Gender-Specific Fashion Poll" ("Okay, so you're a feminist. You don't care what boys think about your clothes. But don't you want to read this anyway?"), *Sassy* made fashion, like feminism, fun—not totalitarian.

It's true that girly fashion was partly a sign of the times. While teen magazine readers have been encouraged to aspire to wearing Prada since the launch of *Teen Vogue* in 2002, in the late eighties and early nineties, "there was a little bit of infantilization running through the culture," according to Daisy Von Furth, who interned with the *Sassy* fashion department in 1989 and later founded the X-Girl clothing label with Kim Gordon. "At the time, it seemed fresh to obsess about coming-of-age stuff." Ravers were wearing diapers. Adult women—like Courtney Love—were wearing kinderwhore dresses, knee socks, underwear as outerwear, and patent-leather Mary Janes. Designers like Anna Sui and Marc Jacobs were appropriating the little-girl look for the runways, so maybe it's no surprise that they were fans of *Sassy*, and *Sassy* was a fan of theirs. (Mary later wrote Jacobs, who had a subscription to the magazine, a letter congratulating him on his infamous and much-derided grunge collection; he wrote back, thanking her for her support.)

And while the magazine may have had to cool it on the gay-friendly sex articles, *Sassy* always had a campy aesthetic. One spread touted the joys of using boy beauty products, and featured a model that could only be described as a butch dyke. Another fashion shoot encouraged a kind of polymorphous, playful sexuality by showing female models dressed up like Bob Dylan. Jacinta based an entire gender-bending photo shoot on Mary's offhand comment to model Amy Smart that she looked just like Axl Rose. Michel Foucault and Judith Butler had made many of the same points about the construction of gender through style in arcane and unintelligible (to the uninitiated, anyway) academic prose; *Sassy* deconstructed gender much more succinctly, and looked good while doing it.

It was this kind of approach that made *Sassy* a cult favorite among gay men, who called it "Sissy." "I think the interest for gay men might have been the sort of outsider's view of the world that *Sassy* had," says fan Richard Wang. "It certainly wasn't mainstream, and sort of had a

'we-aren't-them-and-aren't-they ridiculous' sort of mentality that a lot of gays have. In some way, you know that you're different, special, and probably better than all those fools who make fun of you. But at the same time, you want to be loved by them."

boy-crazy *ym*

Sassy was a hit with readers from the beginning, and by 1990 it was hotter than ever. Its circulation was climbing, its advertisers were back on board, and the other teen magazines were waking up. For *Seventeen*, that meant incorporating some unusual displays of feminist posturing—"Who Says I Have to Have to a Boyfriend?" read one cover line (to which one might like to answer, "Well, *you* do")—and begrudging coverage of non-mainstream celebrities like cartoonist Lynda Barry. Of course, the industry leader also continued to feature model-worship stories and cheerlead prefab boy bands like New Kids on the Block.

But if sixtysomething editor Midge Richardson wasn't hip enough to realize how unhip she was, *YM* saw what was going on. "*Sassy* was another strong competitor," Elizabeth Crow, then president and editorial director for Gruner & Jahr, *YM*'s parent company, noted in an interview. "We were in third place in a three-magazine category, and didn't want to be fourth."

Enter Bonnie Fuller. She's the stuff of magazine legend now—in March 2004, *Vanity Fair* ran a profile chronicling the illustrious editor's successful reign of terror at such publications as *Glamour* and *Us Weekly*—but then she was a thirtysomething Canadian editor who had just nailed her dream job at the hemorrhaging teenybop rag. Bonnie was smart enough to know that her inherent uncoolness would never allow her to tap into youth culture the way that Jane Pratt and her ilk had. Instead, according to Crow, her revamped *YM* would be "all about getting along with, and getting it on with, boys."

It was a funny thing that *Sassy*, like many a high-school girl, could never shed its slutty reputation. In fact, *YM* was arguably a much sexier read—especially in the wake of the right-wing boycott. "The real thing that *YM* delivered was soft porn," says Caroline Miller. "There were all of these stories that were really just beefcake."

YM, under Fuller, was the spiritual younger sister of Helen Gurley Brown's *Cosmopolitan* (in fact, Bonnie would become Brown's successor just a few years later). In Fuller's world, the "Young Miss" was now "Young and Modern," and she was a lot more interested in achieving orgasms than equality. The publication heralded a kind of sexual revolution for young women, but without any attendant feminist critique. Sure, it had a "You go, girl" tone, but it assumed that what you wanted to get was the guy. Or, guys, as the case may be. "Steady relationships are, in a word, confining," one article read, mimicking Brown's mandate that twentysomething single gals should feel free to have as many affairs as they wanted. (It did, however, make a nod to its readers' tender age—or perhaps their parents' conservatism—by tacking on some halfhearted moralizing: "When you have sex with a lot of different men, you become emotionally numbed.") Another piece investigated which partner was responsible for bringing birth control—without any acknowledgment that not all of its readers were sexually active. If this sounds vaguely feminist, the key word is *vaguely*. Unlike *Sassy*, *YM* wasn't mucking around with ideas like "institutionalized sexism." When a girl writes in to complain that boys won't ask her out because she's a bit big in the hips, the male relationship columnist, with no apparent knowledge of teenage girls' propensity toward eating disorders, unhelpfully suggests, "If not being asked out by these guys really bothers you, perhaps you should try to shed a few pounds."

Many, many girls were seduced by *YM*'s covers, which frequently depicted the likes of a shirtless Marky Mark with a halter top–wearing model, the top button of her Express jeans suggestively undone, and by the stories inside, which adhered to Fuller's mandate of "boys, clothes, hair," in the words of *YM* entertainment editor Suzan Colon. *YM*'s circulation almost doubled during Fuller's five-year tenure, and its advertising skyrocketed as well. It became a formidable competitor to *Sassy*, but insiders knew that the new *YM* couldn't have existed without its antithesis. "I want to say that I love *Sassy*," one fan wrote. "I mean, my sister gets the other big teen magazines, and it is so funny. After you came out, I noticed that those guys started to change their format."

the sassiest boys in america

Of course, *Sassy* had always been boy crazy, from an early blurb titled "Why Am I Such a Queer Ball Spazz Head?" in which Andrea reports that she caught Matt Dillon staring at her breasts; to Jane's crush on Keanu Reeves, which was dissected ad nauseum; to Christina's "Cute Band Alert."

But *Sassy* tempered all the swooning with a girl-power tone and a little critique. Instead of deconstructing marriage and interrogating compulsory heterosexuality—that was *Ms.*'s territory—*Sassy* ran feminist-inflected articles on how to ask a guy out. Like other teen magazines, it published pieces titled "How to Flirt" and "Why That Patrick Swayze Poster May Destroy Your Love Life"; unlike other teen magazines, it didn't take its romantic advice too seriously, and didn't assume that getting it on with a jock was your only goal.

And writers could be sure they would hear from readers whose consciousness they had raised when they penned articles that were less ostensibly open-minded: in the infamous April 1990 article "Five Things Never to Ask a Guy," Mike admonishes girls not to pose the questions "What are you thinking?" "Do you love me?" "Do I look fat?" "What would you do if I died?" and "Do you think she's prettier than me?" ("You girls really gotta accept that for every beautiful person, there's one even more beautiful. Just worry about what's inside and don't be such a guy.") It might have seemed like a funny article from a publica-

tion that spent most of its time encouraging girls to say whatever they wanted, but its chauvinism was diluted by the fact that it was authored by a male editor girls were already familiar with, who often took on the pigtail-pulling persona of an older brother. Still, Mike says he got lots of mail that read, "Oh, that's so sexist and you're so close-minded and you're such a Neanderthal."

Another classic *Sassy* relationship article was March 1993's "How to Make Him Want You . . . Bad," which is named after a story that had run in *YM*. In it, Margie Ingall (a staff writer who had been hired in 1990) and Mary Ann try out the inane relationship advice given by *YM* and *Cosmopolitan*. This includes wearing animal prints, which, instead of making Margie look "feral" (presumably a good thing), incite a homeless man to scream "Meow!" The article's last paragraph pretty much sums up *Sassy*'s worldview on men, which is "boys are cute and we like them (unless we hate them) but they're mere dressing on the salad of life."

The magazine regularly tore down the boy-band members and soap-opera stars other magazines were drooling over. (Fan Sarah D. Bunting liked that "they would sometimes call out the famous boys we were all supposed to have crushes on as being tools.") Their coverage of indie bands and indie boys "was giving an alternative to young girls. *Sassy* considered Sebadoh's Lou Barlow to be sexy when everyone was supposed to be looking at the cast of some horrible TV show," says Ann Powers. "It seemed almost political at the time." In retrospect, she says, it may have not been quite that radical. "But at least *Sassy* was presenting different images. Popular music is a template for identity, and sexuality in particular. It's a way young people especially come to figure out who they are as sexual beings; it is really important who they identify with in the pantheon of musical celebrities."

In some way, the magazine helped validate a new kind of American manhood—the kind of guy who would court you with mix tapes, sported Converse Chuck Taylors and shaggy bedhead on his lanky frame, wept over the disappearing rain forest, and had *Backlash* on his bookshelf.

Indie bands were arguably aesthetically superior, but they were also, stereotypically, patently desexualized and more interested in their guitars than their girlfriends—unlike, say, the more explicit songs of mainstream groups like Color Me Badd ("I Wanna Sex You Up"). "These guys are scared to death of girls underneath it all," writes Margie in a February 1994 story titled "The Tormented Boy: An Ethnological Study," covering postmodern boy archetypes like the Disaffected Writer Boy, the Renegade Skater Boy, and, of course, the Soulful Musician Boy. He hangs out in suburban garages and pawnshops selling vintage amps; his mating call is "So, uh, are you going to the Fugazi show?"; his mating ritual is "Strums guitar and raspily sings a lovely (or deliberately not-lovely) song written just for you."

Sassy's readers seemed grateful that the magazine was finally coming clean that courting an indie-rock boy was not without its pitfalls. "Not three days after my boyfriend broke up with me, I received my February *Sassy*," one reader writes. "He is the soulful musician boy to a T! I was totally the strong woman who he said he loved but couldn't commit to."

girl power

"Girls are still understood more clearly as victims of culture and sexuality than as cultural and sexual creators," Naomi Wolf said in *The Beauty Myth*. But *Sassy* reported with a vengeance on creative women who were making a living representing the female experience. The October 1993 issue, for example, includes book reviews of some of the coolest, most pro-girl books of the nineties, all of which would become part of the essential girl-culture canon, including cult hero Francesca Lia Block's *Missing Angel Juan*; Susanna Kaysen's memoir of teen madness, *Girl, Interrupted* (later turned into a movie starring *Sassy* heroine Winona Ryder, who appeared in the magazine long before the other teen mags caught on); Joyce Carol Oates's *Foxfire* (about a girl gang); and the much-maligned Katie Roiphe anti-girl diatribe *The Morning After*, which receives a single star and is referenced with venom in subsequent issues. A record review for Liz Phair's subversive, now classic *Exile in Guyville* exudes, "Orgasmic is not too strong a word to use here."

Blake Nelson, for one, was impressed. In 1990, he was living in Portland, Oregon, when he picked up his girlfriend's copy of *Sassy*. "I remember having this deep feeling like, 'Oh my God, teenage girls are exactly the right thing to be at this exact moment,' " says Nelson. "Like *Sassy*. I had never seen anything so dead-on."

Nelson was working on a novel called *Girl*. "When I named *Girl*, I did it because you weren't even allowed to say *girl*," he says. "And that was the thing that made *Sassy* so great. It was time for girls to just take it away from the super-theoretical and sometimes over-serious and energize it with youth, just have fun with it, and totally be it instead of think it. In a weird way, that was the crowning achievement of all the feminism that had gone before it, none of which ever really got the people involved and never made anyone comfortable. And then *Sassy* comes along and it's just all these girls who are totally cool and will do anything they want."

Nelson was so impressed with the magazine in general and with Christina in particular that he sent her his manuscript. She immediately wrote to him and said she wanted to run an excerpt. In fact, she ran three. Nelson was having trouble getting the book published, until the day when Christina sent him a pile of letters that had arrived at *Sassy*, all from teenage girls, asking where they could buy the novel. "So I immediately ran over to my prospective publisher, dropped them on the desk, and said, 'This is who is going to buy it.' " (Since the book was published in 1995, Nelson has gone on to become a successful young-adult fiction author whose books have been adapted into films by the likes of Gus van Sant.)

"When I was writing *Girl*, the person I was writing it for was Kim Gordon," says Nelson. "I just remember this triumvirate: Kathleen Hanna, Christina Kelly, Kim Gordon—people that were sort of gods of the cultural moment." Hanna was a former stripper and frontwoman for punk feminist band Bikini Kill. She sang about rape and abuse; in concert, she would lift her shirt and scream, "Suck my left one!" Gordon and Sonic Youth had written "Teen Age Riot," a song that would become an anthem of the time. She was skinny and sexy and dyed her hair platinum and wore miniskirts in her forties. She was married to nerd god Thurston Moore. She played the bass and sang in a growl. Thanks to Christina, both Hanna and Gordon made frequent appearances in *Sassy*.

Nelson's obsession with Christina isn't atypical. "Christina, to me, is the key person," says Mike Flaherty. "More than anybody, Christina was the embodiment of the magazine." She was the "soul," says Blake Nelson. Says Mary Kaye, "She felt everything very, very distinctly and she spoke out about it."

In other words, her appeal didn't lie entirely in her exquisite taste; she represented the apotheosis of the teenage girl, and her sensibility was acutely similar to that of her readers. Christina was fearless—even when she was fearful. After Women Aglow's anti-*Sassy* boycott nearly brought the magazine to its knees, Christina verbally flipped the bird to the religious zealots and the namby-pamby advertisers who kowtowed to them by regularly denouncing censorship in her "What Now" column. In one article, she notes that more high-achieving girls than guys have had sex. "What does this mean? I would venture a guess, but I'm afraid I'm going to get in trouble," she says. (Coming from her, it sounds like a taunt, not a concession.) She called out big companies like Domino's and Mennen, who had pulled TV ads when they didn't like the sexual content of certain shows. "I think all of this comes dangerously close to infringement of our constitutional right to free speech. Considering my profession, I consider it particularly scary. And you should, too," she instructed.

"Readers seem to have a love-hate relationship with Christina," *Sassy* acknowledged in one issue. But her incessant ranting was one of the things that kept *Sassy* readers coming back for more. "It felt good and right to delight in Christina's vitriol as we endured the seemingly endless battery of humiliation and frustration that was adolescence," says Rebecca L. Fox in "*Sassy* All Over Again." In one column, Christina asks, "Why is it that MTV shuns real women and only hires inane cartoon characters?" She echoed the thoughts of many of her readers, who then asked themselves: Who was this girl who was so fierce and feminist and fun? Why hadn't anyone told them that this is what they could grow up to be like? "She oozed cool," says fan Julie Gerstein. "Plus, she articulated things in a way that pushed us girls to *also* be articulate, witty, and charming." Christina provided "a model of the kind of adult I wanted to be: hip, concerned, socially active, taking care of business," one fan tells Fox.

The fans may have loved Christina, but not everyone on staff did. The magazine makes constant references to her mood swings, once calling her "Big Meanie" on the masthead. "One intern said that Christina oozed hostility," says Mary. "But she never really scared me. She's very Irish—she's just got that kind of feistiness. She could be really nice." Kim France, an assistant at *7 Days* who took over when Catherine left *Sassy* in 1989, didn't seem to think so—at least not at first. She cried every day her first year at the magazine because she thought Christina hated her. And though they later became close friends—she was even a bridesmaid at Christina's wedding—the two writers' rivalry is apparent in numerous issues. Jane devoted an entire "Diary" to Kim after Kim complained that she was "the invisible staff writer," not pictured as much as Karen and Christina. But many girls were drawn to Kim's smart, serious persona (she was a proponent of volunteerism, international justice, and hip-hop). Christina also terrorized Margie Ingall. "Margie had a really hard time. She and Christina sat next to each other in the back of the room, and they had completely opposite styles," says Mary Kaye. Margie was more of a theatre geek; Christina was an East Village hipster who seemed to relish playing mean girl to the new hire. "Everybody kind of worshipped Christina. They just didn't want to be on her bad side," says Mary Kaye.

Though *Sassy* shared a floor with *Ms.* magazine, Christina was no Gloria Steinem, preaching the gospel of unqualified sisterhood. Why did Johnny Depp and Jennifer Grey break up? "I think he finally got a look at her in broad daylight," she opined. Nor was she Betty Friedan, completely uninterested in the conventional trappings of womanliness. "I have a pathological fear of cellulite and have stooped to purchasing all kinds of ridiculous products to rid myself of it," she admitted in one arguably self-loathing "We Try It." In fact, Christina's complicated version of femininity and feminism heralded a changing of the guard in the women's movement.

the third wave

Parallel to all that was happening at *Sassy* was a resurgence of feminist political activism. In 1991, bands that bridged the divide between independent and mainstream culture—like L7, Pearl Jam, Nirvana, and Hole—teamed up with the Feminist Majority Foundation to present Rock for Choice, a series of benefit concerts intended to give a stalwart issue some cool clout and raise awareness among a younger audience, who had perhaps grown complacent under the protection of *Roe v. Wade*. And in 1992, thousands of people marched for choice in Washington. It was the first major activist event for many women in their late teens and twenties, one that is still popularly understood as marking the inception of feminism's

Third Wave. While the Second Wave focused on gender parity, Third Wave feminism sought to expand the feminist debate about gender and sexuality.

Bad press to the contrary, feminism has never been a one-issue crusade, and the Third Wave's feminist impulse was part of a larger pro–gay rights, anti-racist, multicultural, Democratic political agenda. It was a mandate that *Sassy* pushed at every turn. By 1992, the magazine had become increasingly radical and more overtly political. A reviewer gives a record a single star if she'd "rather work for Clarence Thomas" than listen to it. Bush-bashing becomes omnipresent: Kim slams the then president in a story on America's drug war, and Christina rips him to shreds in a piece on the Gulf War (an article which, incidentally, received more reader mail than any article in the magazine's history). It was as if the *Sassy* staff had forgotten that Women Aglow was watching: the October issue makes no fewer than four pro-choice references. And *Sassy*'s increasingly radical left-leaning political and social agenda wasn't relegated to the "serious" articles—it permeated the entire magazine. Why is there a beauty story on the best cheap makeup? Because "even though a certain president with the initials G.B. says the recession's over, we know better."

But *Sassy* made it seem like identifying as a feminist was a must for any self-respecting teenage girl: "These days you may as well eat dirt as admit to being a feminist . . . We're not embarrassed to admit in print that we all be feminists," proclaimed one staff-written story.

But feminism was not entirely overlooked at *Seventeen*. The magazine even went so far as to run some openly activist pieces, like a profile of National Organization for Women president Molly Yard. Pulitzer Prize–nominated journalist Linda Ellerbee wrote a piece instructing girls to "practice saying these words: 'I am a feminist,' and this time, try to understand what the word means. Feminism means you believe in equality between men and women. Justice. Equal justice for all. And that's all it means." And *Seventeen*'s don't-beat-'em-join-'em brand of feminism realistically mirrored America's shifting middle-class social mores. The magazine had to appeal to 50 percent of the teenage population—girls who were rich and girls who were poor, girls who lived in suburbs and small towns they never wanted to leave. It was one thing for the magazine to advocate equal pay for equal work, and quite another to question the nature of work itself—or, for that matter, the social hierarchy of high school or the intrinsic elitism of sororities.

"Do you need armpit hair to be a feminist?" asked *Sassy* on its June 1992 cover. Mary Kaye didn't think so. "I've never thought twice about whether I was a feminist," she says in the article. "My beef is with really rigid types who have a lot of criteria for what is or isn't a true feminist—you know, shaves her pits? Not. Wears a miniskirt? Not." She also questions "that women-can-have-it-all concept—which sprang up in the late seventies along with the feminist movement . . . It was probably dreamed up by some male advertiser so women would feel inadequate if they didn't do it all." The F-word itself had long been a lightning rod. "People . . . assume you're talking about a humorless, intolerant, rage-filled woman. That's such a stereotype," railed Margie. But she also conceded, "It's true that some of the original feminists from the sixties and seventies were pretty radical and angry—they had more of a reason to be." But by the early 1990s, the staff felt that enough inroads had been made that they could interrogate the movement's ideals in a public forum.

Sassy incited political action in some readers: Constance Hwong declared herself pro-choice in 1992, when she was in eighth grade and learning about the issues surrounding the upcoming election. "I brought an issue of *Sassy* into my social studies class to show my teacher, who seemed impressed at its coverage. I've considered myself a pretty diligent feminist since then, and went on to attend an all-women's college." Fan Amy Schroeder says that the magazine "helped shape my ideas that women are equal to men and that we have the same amount of power—or we should." She went on to major in women's studies in college, and later founded *Venus Zine*, a feminist magazine about women in the arts. *Sassy* was "totally responsible" for all the hours a sixteen-year-old Lara Zeises volunteered for Bill Clinton's presidential campaign. *Sassy* "influenced my politics. I considered myself a feminist from a young age, thanks to an activist grandma," says Caitlin

Kuleci. She "knew that boys were considered better than girls, that racism existed, and that people who were poor had it worse than anybody else. But I lacked a framework with which to understand these things." For her, *Sassy* "was the fertilizer that helped me bloom into my current status as a full-blown dissenter." Rebecca Walker, daughter of author Alice Walker and the cofounder of the Third Wave Foundation, called reading *Sassy* "a political act."

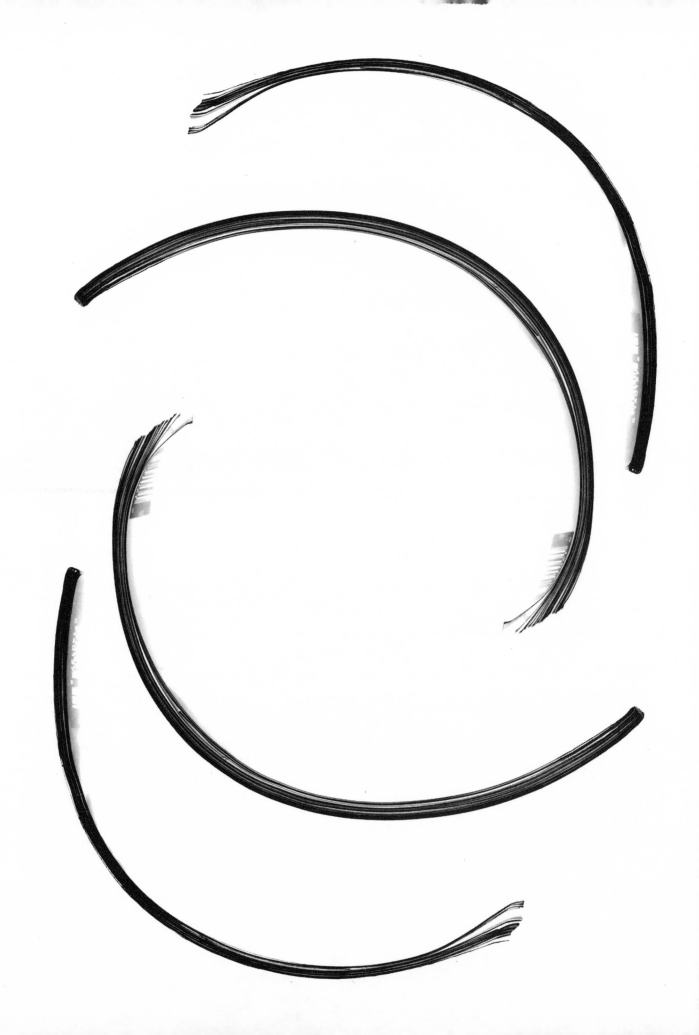

chapter 6

The "Sassy" Ethos

even indier

Ian Svenonius was a philosophy-spouting, pomade-wearing singer in the D.C.-based punk band Nation of Ulysses. Not a vapid jock, or even a sensitive poetic type, he had been a fan of *Sassy* since his friend the singer Lois Maffeo showed him an issue. "I was immediately taken by the writing and the way it didn't condescend to the mythical hoi polloi the way modern journalism condescends to the status quo," he says in his trademark crypto-intellectual rhetoric.

Ian applied for 1990's Sassiest Boy in America Contest (SBIA), a follow-up to the successful Sassiest Girl in America Contest (SGIA)—and won. The impetus behind the competition was one of the staff's truly unifying interests: cute boys.

"I wish I could have applied, but I was too old," laments Calvin Johnson, a longtime fan of teen culture who, in his late twenties at the time, was several years over the cutoff age. But Ian didn't worry about such trifles; he simply lied about his age. (Something he still won't exactly cop to—he said that his band had a policy of being eighteen forever, and therefore when he said he was twenty years old, he was lying older, not younger.) But instead of winning a cash prize and corporate sponsorship, like the Sassiest Girl in America, the SBIA merely got a trip to New York City, a Magic 8 Ball, and "they could go through our collection of CDs that were sent to us that we didn't want," says Christina.

Ian's two days in the city were "like a hot-house forty-eight-hour experiment, like a bio-dome." They sent him to see the band Mindfunk (which Ian dismissed as "not the revolution"), and he went dancing, got his palm read, and had a photo shoot on the Staten Island Ferry. His impression of the *Sassy* office was that magazine people were just like band people. "All of the office talk was about other magazines, just like how bands are obsessed with other bands."

Even though the SBIA contest lacked the hoopla of the SGIA contest, something interesting happened: for at least some indie-obsessed readers, it was far more memorable than its sister contest. Don Smith grew up in the Washington, D.C., area with Ian, and he places a great amount of importance on the ensuing piece. "It was hands down the greatest article in any magazine in the 1990s. They really found the sassiest boy in America—that's the part that was so weird about it—they weren't lying. Normally you say, 'I know people sassier than that.' With Ian it was like the Emmy went to Susan Lucci." He was not only cute and fond of wearing suits, but, as the magazine *Eye* once put it, "probably the only Marxist to be named Sassiest Boy in America." Ian had all of

the cool trappings of a hipster, but without the off-putting attitude.

He also came with a pedigree, having grown up in the 1980s Washington, D.C., punk-rock scene. Ian introduced Christina to the punk scenes in D.C. and Olympia, Washington, and to his indie labelmates on K Records and Dischord. "I was at a party with Calvin Johnson and I said, 'Don't you think it would be cool to have a band named Chia Pet?' " she remembers. "And he was like, 'You guys should start a band named Chia Pet,' and I was like, 'No, I don't have any musical talents,' and he was like, 'Well, that never stopped me.' " The next week Johnson called to say Chia Pet had a show at Bard College, opening up for his band Beat Happening and Ian's Nation of Ulysses—and that they had better start practicing.

Christina's announcement that Chia Pet was about to make their live debut didn't exactly receive the most enthusiastic reception. "I was like, 'Christina, what are you talking about? We don't play instruments. We don't have instruments. We don't have songs. This is just a game we're playing,' " Jessica recalls. "And Christina, being who she is, was determined not to take no for an answer. 'We're doing this and you're going to play bass. You're the bass player.' " She got Karen to share vocal duties with her, and Jane to play the violin. Mary Ann played drums, and Christina's boyfriend Bobby Weeks played guitar. At Chia Pet's first rehearsal, Christina brought in Bobby's brother Eric to teach Jessica bass. (She ended up moving in with him three days later and marrying him a year and a half after that, making Jessica and Christina not only coworkers and bandmates, but sisters-in-law.)

"The Chia Pet shows were so strange," Don Smith remembers. "They were like a *Sex and the City* band—far too sophisticated to be onstage at CBGB's. The standing joke, of course, was 'Don't quit your day job.' But really, no one wanted them to quit their day jobs!" In fact, the band's status as *Sassy* staffers was a bonus. When Johnson booked the Bard show, he just told the promoters that it was a band from New York City. Says Johnson, "When we got there, the two women putting on the show from Bard were like, 'Hey you never told us it was Jane and Christina from *Sassy*!' "

They never played a show outside of New York, but they did record a handful of songs (some produced by legendary indie scenester Kramer), including "Hey Baby," about street harassment (its sarcastic chorus goes "Hey Baby, Hey Baby, You look so good"); a cover of the Human League's "Don't You Want Me Baby"; and "Blind Date," which documents actual blind dates the staff went on. The chorus is "Blind date/don't pick up the phone/pretend you're not home/it's more fun," and the song is set to a bass line lifted directly from Deep Purple's "Smoke on the Water." At one show, Spike Jonze could be found snapping pictures; at another, Ian drew tattoos on everyone with a Sharpie.

The fickle and boy-dominated indie-rock press gave the band a reception ranging from lukewarm ("I thought they were mediocre at best," sniffs one fanzine) to affectionate ("While there is some hype surrounding this *Sassy* magazine–associated band, I am not ashamed of loving the catchy violin and guitar riffs," says zine *Browbeat*.)

zines

Ian also introduced Christina to brother-and-sister duo Don and Erin Smith, who lived in Bethesda, Maryland. Their zine, *Teenage Gang Debs*, was a black-and-white photocopied love letter to sixties and seventies pop culture. They would do things like find Eve Plumb (who played Jan Brady on *The Brady Bunch*) and interview her.

Short for "fanzines," zines are handmade self-published magazines with limited distribution. They became important in the punk scene of the 1970s as a vehicle for writers and were untouched by editors, corporations, advertisers, and censors. Zines have long been a part of underground culture, but *Sassy* was one of the first magazines to give zines mainstream exposure.

Zines were, in keeping with the punk ethos, completely DIY—do-it-yourself. They gave voice to those who were too young, too radical, or too weird to be published elsewhere, and their confessional, stream-of-consciousness style bore a resemblance to *Sassy*'s. Even though zines had been around for twenty years, along with so many aspects of punk culture, the early nineties were a boom time in their popularity.

In the January 1991 installment of "What Now," Christina launched her "Zine Corner." It started after she began receiving zines in the mail (she was the recipient of the greatest amount of random mail of anyone at the magazine, perhaps at least partially because she was seen as the staff member most in touch with underground culture and often featured miscellany that people sent her in the pages of "What Now"). "Zine Corner" soon became "Zine of the Month." (Even *Seventeen* eventually had its own zine column, though it—predictably—sounded like your parents discussing something they heard is cool. Their first "new zine on the block" featured *Cockroach*, which wasn't published by a disaffected teen, but by the daughter of the founder of The Body Shop.)

Christina bought a copy of *Teenage Gang Debs* at the now defunct zine shop See Hear in New York City. Erin Smith was a freshman in college when her publication was featured in "What Now" and, for the next four years, she would go home to her parents' house every weekend and fulfill orders.

Another "Zine of the Month" was *Super Hate Jr.* It was a conceptual zine published by future staff boy Charles Aaron while he was in college. The format was fifty pages of one thing per page that he hated. The reaction to its appearance in "What Now" was immediate. "It was completely insane because I got an avalanche of mail. It was all from teenage girls and gay boys. There were hundreds of them," he says. "The letters were the most incredible thing; they were all so enthusiastic and passionate, and they must have sent these letters out to all the zines they saw in 'What Now.' "

Getting into "Zine of the Month" was both a blessing and a curse. It was, on the one hand, a ringing endorsement of your zine from Christina Kelly, one of the country's arbiters of cool. On the other hand, it might also signal your zine's demise. "People would almost get mad at me because they would get overwhelmed by the orders they got and couldn't do their zine anymore," says Christina. Aaron's zine, for example, sold for two dollars but actually cost about three dollars to make. After sending out so many copies he ran out of money and ended up having to send out cards saying that he couldn't afford to keep it going. They read: "The next time I do a conceptual zine about hatred, I'll keep you in the loop."

riot grrrl

Christina hired Erin Smith as an intern at *Sassy* in 1991 after reading her zine. "Erin consistently wrote smart, witty articles about underground, independent music, and she turned a lot of girls on to fanzines and the idea of DIY culture," recalls D.C. scene veteran Sharon Cheslow, who had discovered punk as a teen girl in the mid-seventies, after reading an article about the Sex Pistols in *Seventeen*. Besides copublishing *Teenage Gang Debs*, Erin Smith was also a key figure, as the guitarist for Bratmobile, in the burgeoning punk/feminist riot grrrl movement. Riot grrrl began that summer, when a group of women from the punk scenes in Washington, D.C., and Olympia, Washington, started to hold meetings—loosely modeled after the consciousness-raising groups of the 1970s—to discuss how to address sexism they had experienced. There had recently been race riots in D.C.'s Mount Pleasant neighborhood. In response, there was a call to start a "girl riot" against a music scene—and society—that didn't give voice to or validate their experiences. The *grrrl* part was a combination of an angry growl and a desire to align themselves with the strong self-esteem of the preadolescent years.

The riot grrrls' frequently heard manifestoes, like "revolution girl style now," found a perfect platform in their zines, like *Girl Germs, Riot Grrrl, Bikini Kill, Jigsaw*, and *Gunk*, which also dealt with seldom-discussed subjects like rape, incest, eating disorders, and sexual harassment. Many of the girls behind these riot grrrl zines were also members of all-girl (or mostly girl) bands whose lyrics echoed the same confessional, confrontational subject matter and who sounded a bit like punkified versions of the women's liberation bands of the 1970s. Zines and bands were a way for girls across the country to meet and share experiences. Besides riot grrrl's overt feminism, perhaps most important was its egalitarian message that you don't have to be special—talented, rich, connected—to be in a band.

When *Sassy* started covering riot grrrl, this relatively obscure punk-rock movement suddenly had an audience of three million impressionable girls who had been reared watching fearless and feisty—but not necessarily self-proclaimed feminist—singers like Madonna, Cyndi Lauper, and Tina Turner on MTV in the 1980s.

"What Now"'s pictures of girls in bands with SLUT and RAPE scrawled across their stomachs (intended to draw attention to women's sexual op-

pression), interviews with band members, and coverage of riot grrrl zines seduced girls across the country. "I would have never known about riot grrrl were it not for *Sassy*," says Julianne Shepherd, who grew up in the isolated town of Cheyenne, Wyoming, in a Mexican Catholic family. She was neither a cowboy nor the class slut she was rumored to be. Inspired by "Zine of the Month," Julianne started her own fanzine called *Lick* that covered music, skateboarding, and "my lady experience." She says, "It wasn't just about fanzines and Bikini Kill. It was bigger than that—it was Third Wave feminism. I clocked time in a cultural island, pre-Internet. If I'd stayed on the path ignorant of feminism, I would probably still be living in Wyoming right now, freebasing something."

The phenomenon of riot grrrl was not ignored by the rest of the media. Soon, sensationalistic articles appeared in *Newsweek* (where it was called "feminism with a loud happy face dotting the 'i' "), *USA Today* ("From hundreds of once pink, frilly bedrooms comes the young feminist revolution. And it's not pretty. But it doesn't wanna be. So there!"), and *Melody Maker*, the British music tabloid ("The best thing that any Riot Grrrl could do is to go away and do some reading, and I don't mean a grubby little fanzine"), all claiming that the movement was juvenile and unimportant.

In the fall of 1992, in reaction to all the negative publicity the women of riot grrrl declared a media blackout. This extended to all corporate-owned TV shows, newspapers, and magazines—

except *Sassy*. In solidarity, a February 1993 "Diary" features a list of things the staff loves and hates, with "riot grrrl media overkill" under "hate." Roni Shapira was interning at *Sassy* at the time. "There was a real sensitivity in the office. The grown women on staff were still very cautious about what younger women in the rest of America were trying to do, and they didn't want to betray that," she says. The first mainstream publication to cover riot grrrls, and to do so positively, *Sassy* had a certain amount of credibility with them and clearly felt a sense of responsibility as well.

But despite *Sassy*'s unconditional support, the riot grrrls hardly embraced their more mainstream sisters. "We weren't punk enough; we were co-opting the scene; we were basically evil," Christina says. "I was like, 'Wait a minute, I met you before you even had a band.'" Even some *Sassy* readers began to take sides, sending Christina hate mail for exposing their counterculture, which angered her further. "'You found out about it from us, and now all of a sudden you're cooler than me?' I'd get so annoyed."

The sad truth is that despite riot grrrls' agitations for equality, the doyennes of the larger underground culture had an elitist attitude toward the kids who learned about indie music, zines, and activism through *Sassy*. "There are some people in the zine community to this day who look down at the kids who were introduced to zines by *Sassy*," says Sarah Maitland, who was one of those teen girls who discovered zines through the pages of "What Now." She started a zine-distribution

business at nineteen, and put out her first zine at twenty. "They don't seem to understand that not everyone lives in a city with a punk scene or a hip coffee shop, or has an older friend or sibling who introduces them to cool new things."

But some of underground culture's biggest enthusiasts were also *Sassy* fans. Guys in their late twenties were psyched to see their indie taste reflected in a magazine where geeks who collected records and wore Jack Purcells were the coolest guys in school.

"The indie-rock world was very interested in youth and the idea of youth," says Ann Powers. This stemmed partly from the fact that many of the up-and-coming cultural creators—whether they were musicians, artists, intellectuals, or magazine editors—were only in their twenties or early thirties themselves. Notoriously awkward in their youth, they were still trying to make sense of their high-school years.

The general obsession with youth culture at the time was part of the reason so many adults read *Sassy*. "Subscribing to a teen magazine totally wasn't embarrassing or weird or a funny fetish. It was part of a general hipness," says Powers. Since so many of the cultural creators were addressing youth in their creations, Powers says, reading *Sassy* "became a tool for a lot of us trying to figure out how to talk to kids in our own work." Powers felt that the existential dilemma of creating and maintaining a pure and idealistic cultural milieu plagued everyone making or commenting on culture in that era. "I can't overemphasize how constant the sense of 'Are we betraying our culture?'

was to the indie generation." The question became how much to popularize it without ruining it.

Christina was painfully aware of this dilemma. The February 1993 issue self-consciously mentions "co-opting" in every "What Now" blurb, like "monthly zine co-opt" and "punk-rock idol co-opting." The staff was savvy enough to know that giving underground media mainstream attention could be viewed as exploitative, but they also knew that they couldn't cover only mainstream culture without alienating their readers, who now looked to them as a guide to the indie scene. Erin Smith, finished with her internship but on the masthead as Washington Bureau chief, guest wrote "Co-opting DC Scene Gossip for Our Own Profit"; the magazine details the riot grrrl scene in that same issue.

It's true that *Sassy*'s indie coverage had a transformative effect on the American underground. The small college town of Olympia, Washington, even felt different because of the attention it received in *Sassy*. In the pages of "What Now," Olympia seemed like the coolest place on Earth. "I have lived here my entire life," Nomy Lamm, a self-proclaimed "fatass, badass jew dyke amputee" activist and writer who published the Olympia-based riot grrrl zine *I'm So Fucking Beautiful*, wrote. "And it never seemed cool to me until I read about it in *Sassy*."

In a way, Calvin Johnson concedes, *Sassy* changed Olympia because in the very early nineties, even though it boasted of being home to many important bands (including Nirvana, who moved there from nearby Aberdeen), none had

been taken seriously yet by a glossy magazine. But Johnson thinks the changes were bigger for *Sassy* than for his hometown: "When *Sassy* discovered this other world and started writing about it, it changed their point of view." He, like many members of the indie world, pinpoints Ian Svenonius as a presence that helped propel *Sassy*'s cultural coverage. "I don't know if Ian knew what he started."

Ian suspects that his introduction to *Sassy* caused some unexpected side effects: he felt like the magazine—particularly the music coverage—became knowing and more self-referential about what it was. "In some ways I feel a little bit of guilt, like I destroyed *Sassy* magazine," he says. "Instead of talking to thirteen-year-old girls, *Sassy* became so conscious of its older audience. I think that made it a little bit harder for them to focus on the real mission of helping girls through the horror of American adolescence."

In a way, Ian is both right and wrong. *Sassy* was certainly guilty of occasionally appearing to be in love with its indie cred. In May 1991's "What Now," Christina even says, "If you read *Sassy* primarily for the zine reviews, check this out." And the spine line of the December 1992 issue reads: "Corporate Zine." It felt like an insular reciprocal world where, for example, *Sassy* would cover L.A.-based zine *Ben Is Dead* in "What Now," and *Ben Is Dead* would frequently name-check *Sassy*, even devoting an issue to a *Sassy* parody.

But for every time an article was about how Halifax, Nova Scotia, would be the next Olympia, there would be an article to counter it, like Christina's story on conquering her fear of escalators, the ever-popular "It Happened to Me" column, and countless features tackling subjects like abortion and how to cope when your best friend commits suicide. Despite its indie cred, *Sassy* never lost focus of the day-to-day travails of teenage life.

According to fan Rita Hao, part of what made *Sassy* so appealing to all of its fans was that, "You could read zines for underground stuff, or you could read *Seventeen* for totally mainstream stuff, but it was really kind of weird to read something that had both, which I think was what made it such a seductive read both for people who love zines ('Wow! I can like *90210!*') and for people who were primarily *Seventeen* readers (like me, you know, 'Wow, what's this crazy super-8 shit?')."

do-it-yourself

Sassy encouraged girls not to just consume culture—be it indie or mainstream—but to create it themselves, whether it was by publishing a zine, forming a band or indie label, or becoming an activist. Underground culture had always been covered, however briefly, in hipper glossy magazines like *Spin* or *Details* but, before *Sassy*, no one had ever thought to cover it for teenage girls. *Sassy* single-handedly shifted the paradigm of what kinds of things were cool for a teenage girl to do; in the pages of *Sassy*, being a drummer or a zine publisher was way better than being on the prom committee.

Sassy's concept of DIY was not limited in scope. Beyond the magazine's boosterism of

zines, indie music, and riot grrrl, it had long touted making one's own clothes and beauty products as not just thrifty, but chic as well. *Sassy* not only told its teen readers that they could do anything they wanted, but also how to do it. Articles like "Kicking Out the Jams," on how to start a band; "How to Have a Job in Music and Be Female"; and "You Can So Be a Writer" featured words of wisdom and practical advice from successful women, proving to *Sassy* readers that their goals were attainable. Even if you didn't specifically want to start a band or become a writer, *Sassy* assured you that those options—and more—were there for you. The very act of demystifying access was reminiscent of both Second Wave feminism and the DIY ethos of punk.

All of *Sassy*'s talk about independence had a major impact. "It was my first introduction to DIY that did not involve sewing, canning, or making crafts," says Caitlin Kuleci, who grew up Mormon in Utah and always felt like an outcast. It was "as if everyone had gotten some sort of rule book at birth, which I was mysteriously born without. Nothing really spoke to me, not just as a teenage girl but as a teenage girl who was pissed off and annoyed at the world." That changed when Caitlin discovered *Sassy* through two non-Mormon friends of her sister. "My world was a chorus of no—no sex, no hair dye, no short skirts, no music with cuss words, no causing a scene—no, no, no. *Sassy* was the first time I heard yes in a way I understood—yes to college for learning instead of just husband-hunting, yes to speaking your mind, yes to being smart and being proud of it. It was a yes I desperately needed to hear." Maria Cincotta remembers, "Sassy definitely made me want to start a band. I actually started my first band at age fifteen with a bunch of other Sassy readers." Irene Huangyi Lin, in an article on her Web site called "Sassy Girls Are Still Around," agrees. "Sassy taught me that teenage girls were supposed to be creative, outspoken, and independent instead of mindless, unquestioning consumers."

Some Sassy readers, like Alice Tiara, created a sort of lifestyle around Sassy's DIY cheerleading. Besides being introduced to indie rock in Sassy, Alice proudly recounts writing a column in her school newspaper "in which I deplored the conformity of the Gap and the apathy of my fellow students"; making a T-shirt that read HOMOPHOBIA IS QUEER (and wearing it, in true Sassy fashion, with ripped-up fishnets and a kilt); and protesting a policy that required girls and boys to wear graduation gowns segregated by color. She notes that although she and her friends did not succeed at that one, they did get a "statement about gender equality" read at graduation.

"One thing the religious right didn't really count on when they freaked out about sex in the first few months of the magazine was that we ended up being much more subversive when we couldn't talk about sex," Margie has said. "Telling girls to be independent thinkers—that's much scarier than telling girls how to give a blow job."

The Sassy ethic of doing it for yourself is a direct descendant of a very American notion of nonconformity. Both Sassy's readers and editors, for the most part, were members of Generation X,

derided at the time for being low-achieving slackers. In fact, "slacking" was a new, different definition of achievement, where meaningful work and following your bliss trumped wage-slave jobs. Sassy was certainly an arena where following your bliss was encouraged. At the same time, as high-school students, Sassy's readers were studying the American ideals of civil disobedience under the likes of Walt Whitman, Ralph Waldo Emerson, and Henry David Thoreau. Even as parents and teachers were asserting their authority, Sassy was reinforcing the idea that girls should question adults' decisions and power.

In essence, Sassy was teaching girls to be hip. In his history of the subject, Hip, John Leland writes, "If hip is a form of rebellion—or at least a show of rebellion—it should want something. Its desires are America's other appetite, not for wealth, but for autonomy." In the past, if it had mostly been men (the Beats, et al.) who won this independence, this time there was a feminist twist.

community

Hip, of course, is about status. Sassy was the first magazine to give being a nerdy girl its own cultural cache. Laura Padilla says that "Sassy appealed to the teenage snobbery that I affected . . . Made me feel smarter and cooler than the girls who read YM." Melody Warnick remembers, "I had this sense of myself as being really different, and a whole lot cooler, than the other people in my high school. And Sassy affirmed that for me.

It made me feel hip, smart, a little rebellious, and alternative." *Sassy* reassured girls that there were other people out there who existed on the fringe of mainstream teen culture.

In fact, according to *Sassy*, being considered a loser at your high school (whether currently attending or in the possession of a diploma) was practically a badge of honor. In "Popular People Are as Insecure as You," one of many stories designed to soothe the battered egos of its fragile, sensitive readers, Kim deconstructs the cool crowd. The piece lists reasons *Sassy* readers should stay on society's sidelines because, otherwise, "you're forced to conform," "you have to play dumb," "you're undoubtedly elitist," and "your chances of being cool later are inversely related to your popularity level in high school."

Julie Gerstein—who bonded with her best friend when they first met, over how much they wanted to be *Sassy* editors when they grew up (alas, she didn't get her wish to work at *Sassy*, but she does work in magazines today)—suspects that the girls and boys who read *Sassy* "felt a certain sense of angst-fueled boredom and insecurity that made them feel like outsiders in some way or another. It's something that's permeated a lot of different subcultures—be it riot grrrl or punk rock or whatever—the idea that 'what we do is secret.' Even if it's not literally secret, there is a secret language, or knowledge that defines one as either in or out of the club. And in that way, *Sassy* created a legion of girls and boys all speaking a similar outsider language—infused with wit, snark, and sincerity."

Being saved by the magazine from her dull hometown is a story nearly every *Sassy* fan tells. They were girls who Constance Hwong describes as "quirky, witty types with a penchant for Dorothy Parker, thrift-store clothes, and Doc Martens," or who Alice Tiara calls "the edgy alternative girls, the feminist girls. Later we'd be the ones who gave political speeches in class about censorship and wore our hair in pigtails while snarling and looking fierce in between going to debate tournaments and doing physics homework." *Sassy* reassured its readers that there were plenty of girls just like themselves out there (this kind of fringe-leaning teen would later become a commodified persona, perhaps thanks to *Sassy*).

Certain magazines are successful for aiding readers in finding kindred spirits, but publications like *The New Yorker*, *Vanity Fair*, or *Spy* are often for the financial or cultural elite and serve the purpose of reaffirming their readers' rarified status. "*Sassy* was for a totally disenfranchised group—teen girls—or, rather, double-disenfranchised, since these girls also felt like they didn't fit in," says Professor David Abrahamson, who also thinks that *Sassy* helped create a certain "liberated spirituality," or an edict to live one's life as honestly as possible.

The girl who read *Sassy* was reluctant to go off the grid in terms of media, so having one foot in mainstream America was still important to her because, as Ann Powers theorizes, "It's a very rare person who is confident and informed enough in high school to be able to completely reject mainstream pop culture. If you're going to live in an alternative media universe, it takes quite a bit of effort." The *Sassy* reader was also equally alienated and passionate, culturally literate and adventurous, and interested in self-expression.

Sassy was never meant to be a niche magazine—its circulation was high and its distribution was nationwide. But so effective was its combination of mainstream and alternative culture that there were definitely nonbelievers in the industry who mistook *Sassy* for a publication for a smaller group. "I remember someone saying to me on an ad-sales call once, 'Isn't *Sassy* just for alienated teenagers?' And I said, 'An un-alienated teenager —that's not a lot.' What teen-ager doesn't feel alienated?" says Jane. (Anyone who has ever noted the frequency with which *The Bell Jar* appears on teen girls' bookshelves would likely agree.)

And the sense of community that girls felt with the magazine wasn't just mental. In fact, girls tried to interact with the magazine—and with one another—physically. They sent letters to people who appeared in the magazine, they interned at *Sassy*, they met one another at thrift stores or at shows for indie bands they read about in *Sassy*: they sought one another out, which took a lot of effort in the pre-Internet age. Now it's much simpler for magazine readers (or people with any common interest) to connect with one another; every magazine has a Web site with online forums, Q&As with staff members, and email addresses for each department. If anything, these days such efforts to connect readers to a magazine work as marketing gimmicks. But with *Sassy*, the evolution of a community of readers wasn't some-

thing the staff planned; according to Christina, "It was this thing that sort of evolved."

Sarah Crichton says she thinks her readers felt similarly connected to *Seventeen*, but "*Sassy* was able to triangulate [their audience]." In other words, they responded both to the magazine and to one another. "Part of it was that you had the girls who had not felt like they had belonged to anything, so they found one another. There was this sentiment that, 'I'm sure as hell not *YM*, I'm sure as hell not *Seventeen*, but I'm not *Cosmo*, so what am I?' "

In reality, the majority of *Sassy*'s audience was not urban hipsters. "Most of our readers were in the middle of the country. I mean, we're talking about Pocatello, not cool places," says Karen. (In fact, according to *Sassy*'s marketing kits, their circulation mirrored the U.S. population almost exactly, with 22 percent of their readers in the Northeast, 21 percent in the West, 29 percent in the South, and 28 percent in the Midwest.) But *Sassy* brought cool to rural and suburban girls in the form of music, books, movies, and other cultural ephemera in a genuinely exuberant way. "And I think that's part of it, too; people who didn't live in urban centers are easily alienated by magazines that they perceive for even a second as condescending to them, not including them," says Karen.

the reader-produced issue

In early 1990, the staff decided to take the idea of letting real girls get involved with the magazine a step further. They held a contest in which readers could apply for positions at the magazine, culminating in the first reader-produced issue (RPI). Both the business and editorial sides take credit for the idea. Either way, according to Mary Kaye, "It was really just for the reader, so that they would know that there was a chance they could be a part of [*Sassy*]."

Summer Lopez was the editor in chief of the first RPI. She had been a *Sassy* reader since the premier issue and applied for every single job in the special issue (as did Atoosa Rubenstein, who was, according to Mary, "rejected for every position," but was eventually accepted as an intern at *Sassy*; she later became the editor in chief of *Seventeen*). Summer was studying geometry in summer school when her mother got the call from Mary Kaye about the job. When she heard the news, on a pay phone at school, she fell down and dropped the phone, crying and laughing. She had two weeks to compose herself and get to New York.

"There were some bumps in the road," Summer remembers. Like figuring out exactly what her role would be. The reader staff was small, and only a few of them got to fly to New York (most worked long-distance). But the RPI was a success and became an annual event at *Sassy*.

Tali Edut, a reader from Michigan, was the art director of the second RPI, which had the largest number of readers working out of the New York office and the greatest political bent, which extended to the quiz, "How Much Do You Know About Rape?" a stark contrast to the usual light-hearted fare like "Are You Ridiculously Roman-

tic?" or "Are You a Slacker?" The cover was to be a shot of two models, one African American and the other Asian. But they were asked to make one addition to the shoot, Tali remembers. "They made us put a blond white chick on the cover. They were afraid we would alienate the white readers. And we were all like, *'Come on.'*" It should be noted, though, that the sole model on the cover of the 1992 RPI was African American—something the editorial staff decided to green light despite the publishing side's warnings that doing so would jeopardize sales. (In fact, Tali and her twin sister, Ophi, went on to found *HUES—Hear Us Emerging Sisters*—a feminist magazine with a more overtly multicultural mission than that of *Sassy*.)

For the last RPI, Ethan Smith—the staff boy who replaced Charles Aaron, who had written for the first RPI—became the chaperone. "In retrospect it seems so absurd that a twenty-two-year-old would be in charge of ten kids between [the ages of] fifteen and twenty-five," he laughs. He took them to East Village coffee shops (they were too young to go to bars) and to Maxwell's, a club in Hoboken, New Jersey, to see Unrest play. One night they were hanging out in pre–chain store Times Square and Ethan realized that he alone was responsible for a group of kids whose parents had signed release forms that were only two pages long—an impossibility in today's litigation-happy age. But it was in keeping with *Sassy*'s faith in young people. As Ethan points out, "At the time it didn't seem that abnormal, in a way. It was sort of typical of the whole *Sassy* experience, where they would put a recent college graduate in charge of all these minors and just see if it would work itself out. And it did."

Beyond simply getting the chance to work at their favorite magazine, the RPI provided readers with the opportunity to meet up with fellow *Sassy* obsessives, a crew that was not made up of typical high-school girls. "We were fifteen-year-old kids comparing notes on Camille Paglia," says Roni Shapira, who filled in for Christina on the second RPI. "Though we were all really different, we all had the sense that we had found our people." There was even some talk that the staff was a bit less cool than this highly discerning, authenticity-obsessed group had thought (perhaps it was hard for them to live up to their *Sassy* personas). But for Shapira, it was an experience in which she could meet and bond with Christina and interview singer Henry Rollins (with whom she remained pen pals for a few months). When her issue came out, she was called into her high-school guidance counselor's office about a PFLAG (Parents and Friends of Lesbians and Gays) scholarship, the counselor probably assuming that such an odd girl must be a lesbian. "*Sassy* branded me in the eyes of my college counselor," Shapira laughs. It was further proof, perhaps, that outside of *Sassy*, it was the rare adult who got it.

But not everyone lucky enough to work on the RPI felt like they had found their community. Lara Zeises replaced Mary Clarke as beauty editor of the second RPI. She had spent the entire year practicing her writing—penning fake articles, short stories, and plays—so that when the call

went out for the second RPI she would be ready. When she found out she had the job, it felt like the best thing that had ever happened to her.

But when she got to New York, she felt like she didn't fit in with the other girls because she "didn't wear [her] subversiveness on the outside." Most of the girls who were chosen were the misfits at their own high schools, but when they took over *Sassy*, suddenly Zeises was the outcast. At fifteen, she was one of the younger RPI staffers. One girl would always ask Zeises's opinion because, as Zeises puts it, "she thought I was a more typical magazine reader. She meant it almost as an insult." Furthermore, her RPI editor rewrote one of her articles, an interview with a Cover Girl model, because it wasn't sarcastic enough.

Zeises felt spurned outside the *Sassy* offices as well. Every RPI had a slumber-party vibe, and there were lots of late-night conversations at the hotel. One night someone got hold of some alcohol, and everyone was drinking. They started playing the pussy game—taking one word of a song title and replacing it with *pussy*. The game ultimately became about trying to make Zeises say the word. She wouldn't—and as a result was branded the issue's token goody-goody. "I never felt the same about *Sassy* after that. I felt like *Sassy* was about celebrating individuality, but to those girls it was about conforming to some standard of nonconformity," she laments. "I wanted to be cool enough to hang with the kids I considered cool. And I was hurt when those same kids rejected my attempts."

"At some point, the typical *Sassy* girl became a

smugly superior alterna-chick," says Zeises, who now writes young-adult fiction. "I was never actually cool enough to read *Sassy*. I listened to show tunes and wore leggings until my freshman year in college. But I was smart and funny and subversive in my own way."

the dark side

Zeises is not the only fan who feels betrayed. John Leland calls hipness "a strategy in the face of terror"—and the high-school years can no doubt be terrifying. But this idea of hipness was a strategy that girls could turn on one another. *Sassy* paid a lot of lip service to the notion of being yourself, but this message felt to some like it came with the caveat that you could be yourself as long as your true self was really cool according to the magazine's standards. "*Sassy* had its low points. While they championed the black-wearing, artistic non-cheerleader, they did it at the expense of the bubbly yet still smart cheerleader," says fan Liz Menoji. In the early years, *Sassy*'s endless stories excoriating beauty pageants and sororities felt like a huge victory for girls whose worst nightmare was playing the pop tart. But sometimes *Sassy* cast not just the institutions, but also the people who participated in them, as the enemy.

And while the staff often boasted of their open-mindedness and encouraged similar behavior from the magazine's readers, *Sassy* could, in fact, be really judgmental in its devotion to this ideal. The staff singled out *90210* star Shannen Doherty as an object of their derision because of her hammy acting, but also because of her Republican leanings. *Sassy*'s staff was certainly entitled to (and for the most part beloved for) their political views, but for a magazine that celebrated the liberated, experimental teen-girl worldview, this could be seen as a touch of tunnel vision.

But you weren't immune even if you were a card-carrying member of the Democratic party who volunteered at Planned Parenthood and had her sights set on a decidedly liberal East Coast college. As Zeises attests, in the later years *Sassy* could equate how you looked and what you listened to with the kind of person you were—and that's where things became increasingly problematic. There's Chloë Sevigny, for instance, who was always held up as a paragon of sassiness in the magazine—but it seems as if her sassiness was derived entirely from her look, as seen in a February 1993 "About Face" column, where she was praised for cropping her ultra-long hair in favor of a hip, Mia Farrow–esque pixie cut. Similarly, a September 1991 article called "Primal Beauty" celebrates body piercings (including Jane's nose ring) and tattoos used as marks of individualism. The unspoken idea was that if you didn't conform to these supposedly daring fashion and beauty statements, which were associated with *Sassy*'s liberated paradigm, then you must not be cool.

The question of whether they were cool enough for their favorite magazine still looms large in some readers' minds. "I was a girl banished into not just the suburbs but the outskirts of the suburbs, and had access to very little," says reader Kendra Gaeta. "I had a single mom and my life didn't feel urban enough to identify with what was cool, nor was I privileged enough to buy what I was seeing." *Sassy* was a very middle- and upper-class magazine—a junior version of the bourgeois bohemian culture popularized by David Brooks in his book *Bobos in Paradise: The New Upper-Class and How They Got There*—in some ways more so than *Seventeen*, which often ran features on ways to make money over the summer or on proper dress for your first job, and routinely featured less elite colleges than those discussed in *Sassy*'s pages. For all its liberal leanings and efforts to show a more multicultural view of teen life, the magazine still celebrated a white indie culture whose priority was never about making ends meet.

In a certain way, this kind of underground culture that *Sassy* was so enamored of was in reach and thus inclusive—thrift-store clothes, cheap cups of coffee, and used record bins were hardly expensive or hard to come by—but for the average self-conscious teen girl, it might be difficult to take on that lifestyle without ridicule. Marla Tiara, who grew up in a small town in Massachusetts and was a *Sassy* intern, always skipped the fashion pages. "I thought I couldn't wear that stuff. If I wore anything that wasn't a Benetton rugby shirt, I would be made fun of for five weeks. In high school I kept my head down and wanted to blend in."

And *Sassy* encouraged its readers to see the world in similarly black-and-white terms. Like Zeises's experience with her fellow RPI staff, some girls felt that they couldn't live up to the standard, and felt like exiles from yet another community. And some of them blame *Sassy* for condoning this girl vs. girl behavior. While girls revered *Sassy* for telling the truth about celebrities—however unflattering that truth might be—the magazine's own inherent cattiness encouraged a similar outlook from its readers. And while it could be argued that prefab idols like Tiffany, Milla Jovovich, and Tiffani-Amber Thiessen were worthy of being knocked down, it could also be argued that all three were young girls, possibly young girls with less self-confidence and smarts than *Sassy* readers, and more easily molded. And there's no excuse, really, for some of Christina's comments. "I wonder what that sweet little Balthazar Getty sees in that dirty old tattoo-covered Drew Barrymore?" she writes in a February 1991 issue of "What Now." Even Kim Gordon was less than impressed, noting in a May 1991 *Spin* article, "I found this knock at little Drew a little uncool."

The irony of it all is that *Sassy* was begun as an alternative to *Seventeen*'s blond, bland uniformity. But to some readers that nonconformity became a new uniformity. "I wasn't represented in these pages," says Rita Hao. "The staff was all hanging out in the East Village and dyeing their hair. But just because I was trying to go to law school didn't mean I wanted a boring life."

Many *Sassy* readers feel like they haven't lived up to the magazine as adults, as if anything short of adopting Ethiopian babies, starting an all-girl noise band, or working in publishing in New York would live up to *Sassy*'s standards of cool adult living. "I wanted to learn how to grow up and not make compromises—how to stay true to myself," says Hao. What she didn't want was a new, equally confining standard to live up to.

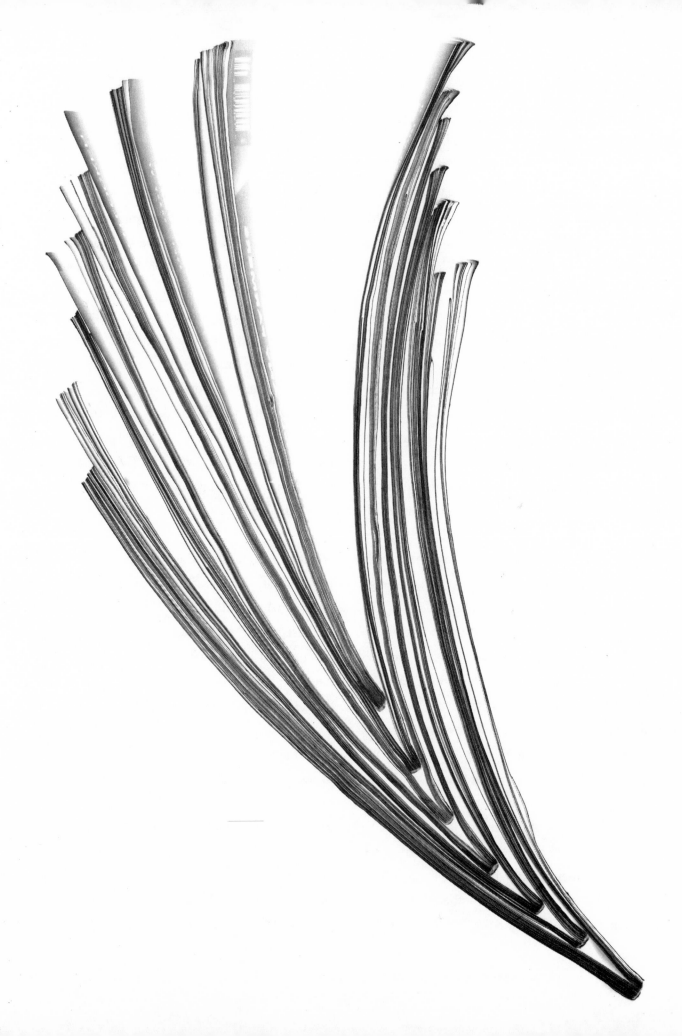

chapter 7

The Fall

the talk show

. . . .

When a magazine succeeds in selling a distinct paradigm to its readers, like *Sassy* did, there's always the temptation to expand the brand into a lifestyle. *Sassy* had a perfume (not exactly a hit with their much-needed beauty advertisers, who resented the competition); binders, T-shirts, and fanny packs emblazoned with the *Sassy* logo; and a behind-the-scenes video called *Even More Sassy*. The magazine's conspiratorial tone and young, photogenic staff lent themselves well to other media, so

it was only a matter of time before Hollywood came calling. An agent at Creative Artists Agency, Bruce Vinokour, pitched a pre-MTV *Real World* to the magazine. The series was to be a combination of sitcom and reality, revolving around a young girl who had come to New York to intern at *Sassy*. The staff would have guest spots on the show, which also promised to have very earnest, un-*Sassy*, after-school special "serious messages," as *Sassy*'s executive vice president and publisher Bobbie Halfin remembers.

Not only would a TV show be a good way to give *Sassy* a wider audience, but it would also elevate Jane's status as an arbiter of teen taste. This wasn't something she was opposed to. "She was trying to become a celebrity, and becoming more enamored with celebrities. Which were two things that were very un-*Sassy*, with a capital *S*," says Mike, noting that Jane had acquired numerous new famous friends. She appeared on the game show *To Tell the Truth* and was filmed getting her nose pierced on *First Person with Maria Shriver*. She was even rumored to be taking acting lessons. The proposed *Sassy* sitcom never got off the ground, though; negotiations fell apart when Jane failed to show up to an important meeting (a meeting Jane says she knew nothing about).

But that didn't mean Jane didn't want to be on TV. In February 1992, with the blessing of publicity-hungry Halfin and Lang, Jane gave up her day-to-day duties at *Sassy* to start her own talk show, simply called *Jane*, on Fox—something that, in the early-1990s heyday of Sally Jesse Raphael and Jenny Jones, was a popular career path. Jane wanted a new challenge, and the magazine's owners thought it would be good PR for *Sassy*, whose newsstand sales were declining. (Lang was happy to oblige; according to Jane, he was to receive half of her host salary.) Lang, however, claims this wasn't true. For *Sassy* fans who had a hard time waiting each month for a new issue, the prospect of having Jane's talk show—a living, breathing version of the magazine—in their homes every day after school was thrilling.

Except it didn't quite work out. *Jane* tackled *Sassy*-esque topics like young women and AIDS

and gay teens coming out of the closet. But it also had more sensationalistic themes like "X-Rated Ways I Worked My Way Through College," "I'm Not Stupid, I'm Just Blond," and "Men Only Date Me for My Big Breasts." Unlike *Sassy*, *Jane* was not a critical success. One writer in *The Village Voice* called a piece about the show "The De-*Sassy*fication of Jane Pratt." In New York's *Newsday*, her show was dismissed as "doing everything that's been done before on the afternoon talk shows—except it's for teenagers." And Jane was called the "biggest hypocrite in a business filled with hypocrites." Julie Gerstein remembers watching the show and finding it "sort of embarrassing. What was she thinking?" Jane, such a natural writer and editor, came across as not only stiff and uncomfortable on television, but also as a phony.

Jane, who was accustomed to having creative control over everything that went into the magazine, suddenly had to answer to Fox executives. "I really had hardly any say," she says in her own defense. But the show's saving grace was that at the very end of each episode, there would be a quick shot of the cover of the latest issue, which would spike newsstand sales. "It deserved to have a bad rating but they were actually good," says Jane. Nonetheless, the Fox show was cancelled after just one season. But the magazine was doing so well that in March 1993 Jane's new show, called *Jane Pratt*, debuted on Lifetime. The general feeling among Jane, her agent, Lang, and Bobbie was that Lifetime—even though it had a smaller po-

The Fall

tential audience—would produce a show that was not exploitative and was more in keeping with the *Sassy* message. It tried hard, even having a riot grrrl show featuring zine editor Jessica Hopper, Kim Gordon, Christina Kelly, and the (decidedly *not* riot grrrl) Dutch indie band Betty Serveert. But it didn't repair Jane's image as a D-list talk-show host, and ran for only five months. "I dated someone who said that you were doomed if you go on that show. You fail the second you go onto the show," remembers Jennifer Baumgardner.

"The talk show was like a nightmare," says Jane. "I would wake up and go, 'I had this horrible dream that I was hosting Oprah's show.' Only it was true. It wasn't a dream. Everything in me was fighting it, and you could see that when you saw it. I thought it was undermining everything I had built at *Sassy*." Halfin echoes the sentiment: "The whole thing was horrible."

The unlikely beneficiary of Jane's misfortune was actress Rikki Lake, who took over Jane's spot on Fox. Lake's show was not a critical success, but was on the air for eleven seasons. Later, she approached Jane at a party. "She came up to me and said, 'I'm so glad you left and kept your integrity, because I made a whole lot of money,' " says Jane, laughing.

The talk show's failure had a devastating effect on morale at the magazine. "We shouldn't have even tried," says Lang. "When the show finally went away it was a big let-down, and it was kind of like we were over, the good days were behind us."

resentment

With Jane basically M.I.A. during the run of the talk show, Mary Kaye became the de facto editor, and Christina was promoted as well. Under Mary Kaye, *Sassy*'s office politics heated up. "Jane was very good at being the good cop. I didn't want to be the bad cop, but you have to get the articles done. The staff all hated me," she says. Even the way the office was set up contributed to the tension, with Mary Kaye in the back and everyone else up front. "Every time I'd walk into that room, everyone would stop talking. It felt like high school," she says. Some staffers were loyal to her, while others didn't like her editing approach. She felt so embattled that she even went so far as to hire her mother as her assistant. Mary Schilling, a Lucky Strike–smoking, no-nonsense woman who regaled the office with tales of youthful love affairs with Canadian Mounties, was an effective shield for her daughter.

Jane was able to keep her editor in chief title, and her name still signed off each month's "Diary" column, but the reins of the magazine had definitely been handed over. Attentive readers began to notice that lists and guest writers began to dominate Jane's column. "For some reason I don't remember Jane Pratt as strongly," says fan Annie Tomlin. "She was definitely a presence, but it always seemed like the magazine was produced collaboratively." Jane's absence from the magazine was *Sassy*'s dirty little secret. And certainly, from its inception, Jane had gotten most of the attention in the media. Upon the launch of her talk show, Jane was the subject of features in *Interview, Newsweek,* and *New York* magazine. "The fact that the media bought that Jane was still running the magazine was more shocking to me than when they asked me to run it. I don't blame this on Jane; it was just funny that people thought she could do both of these things at the same time," Mary Kaye remembers.

Resentment had been building among the staff for years. "The problem really started for me when she left to do the TV show," says Mary Kaye. "There was this incredible love-hate thing for Jane because she got all the credit." With Jane gone at her talk show, the rest of the staff was taking on more and more responsibility without any kind of recognition, and they were getting seriously disgruntled. "We felt like we were just as integral to the magazine as she was," says Christina. "And I remember feeling like, 'Why is it always about Jane?' Because she was this mini-celebrity."

To be fair, Jane's behavior during this time was actually normal business practice. At any other magazine, it's accepted that the editor in chief makes more money and gets the accolades (they also take the fall; they're the first to be fired if a magazine is deemed unsuccessful). Furthermore, from the 1960s on, magazine editors like Helen Gurley Brown at *Cosmopolitan,* Anna Wintour at *Vogue,* Jann Wenner at *Rolling Stone,* and Tina Brown at *Vanity Fair* were becoming celebrities in their own right. Jane was ascending as a young, name-brand editor. "I think Dale looked at Jane as irreplaceable, and we really made her

hot," says Bobbie Halfin, who, along with Lang Communications's publicist Andrea Kaplan, promoted Jane in the media. There was no way Lang was going to take Jane's name off the masthead or hire a new editor in chief just to pacify mutinous employees.

Still, Jane was one of the youngest members of the staff and *Sassy* had, as Mike puts it, "an inner sense of egalitarianism" about the process of putting together a magazine. After all, wasn't the fact that *Sassy* was such an overtly collaborative effort part of what made the magazine stand out in the first place? "I don't envy them," Jane says, of her staff. "I was getting the credit for a lot of the work they were doing. But that's sort of how it is: the editor in chief gets the attention. But at the time I guess I didn't know that, and I felt bad, and I felt like I was exploiting them."

dale lang

After just four years of publishing, *Sassy* was not just a hot up-and-coming magazine, but an unmitigated success. But it wasn't easy to keep that up. Unlike larger publishing companies, Lang Communications lacked the funding to pay for things like preferential newsstand placement, mall tours, advertising, or direct-mail campaigns that could sustain or bolster the magazine's success. *Sassy* also wasn't Lang's highest priority; that would be *Working Woman,* Lang's biggest revenue producer. And ironically, as *Sassy* was making its financial comeback, *Working Woman* was on its way down, taking all the other magazines in Lang's stable with it, partly a casualty of that era's recession.

Lang needed an infusion of cash to run the company. But "Cute Band Alert" apparently wasn't as beloved on Wall Street as it was in the East Village. "I dealt with different investment banks, and these guys were the worst. You couldn't get a banker to understand *Sassy* at all," says Lang. He found an investment bank that promised them money. "At the last minute they said, 'No, we're not going to do it.' And I wasn't really willing to just accept that, and I really got in their face and said, 'Why? What turned you off all of a sudden?' It turned out it was *Sassy*. They did not want to invest in a crazy teen magazine." Since the "crazy teen magazine" was pinpointed as the problem child in the Lang Communications family, it wasn't long before the powers-that-be started thinking that *Sassy* might need to be sold in order to save the rest of the company.

The truth might have been that the problem lay less with *Sassy* and more with Lang himself. Lang didn't command a great deal of respect in the industry. While he had been an important publisher in the 1980s and early 1990s, he was becoming known as a bumbling businessman, and some of his practices were considered suspect. (There were rumors that Lang was falsifying circulation for some of his publications.) As Jane's talk show was failing, her relationship with Lang began to deteriorate. He wanted to trademark her name so that no one else could use it. "I think somebody tried to use the name 'Jane' and I asked my lawyer to set up a copyright on it, so we'd own the name Jane, and he couldn't do it," says Lang. It was a power struggle with no easy resolution: Lang had helped make Jane into a celebrity, and with her newfound star status she wanted to achieve greater fame than his relatively small company could manage.

Life at Lang Communications kept getting worse, not that it was lavish to begin with. This was a company where, as Mike says, "We had to fight to get a fax machine." *Sassy* didn't have any kind of message system for its office phones—there wasn't even a receptionist, so if staffers were in a meeting or out to lunch and missed a call, well, too bad—they missed the call. Instead of donating to charities the money they made selling beauty-product samples, like most magazines do, Mary had the idea to put aside the cash toward an answering-machine fund.

Sassy's Christmas parties were also tellingly indicative of Lang's bare-bones approach. There was an elegant soiree when Lang first purchased *Sassy*. "He was like, 'I'll keep the bar open for another hour,' and we were like, 'Wow, you actually may be Daddy Warbucks,'" Kim says, smirking. The next year, Lang offered ad space to a boat company called Spirit of New York in exchange for a free party. There were two other Christmas parties going on, so the *Sassy* staff was stuck in the basement of the boat. The food was free, but the drinks were another matter. "You had to pay for cocktails," says Andrea. There were waiters ambling up to the staff singing, "Ooh, Spirit, working aboard the cruise." Andrea remembers wondering, "Do you want to stop singing and come give us some drinks?" The next year was the nadir. The holiday party was held in the conference room, and the sole refreshment was an Entenmann's cake, served straight from the box.

end of days

Given the obstacles, *Sassy* somewhat miraculously found itself celebrating its fifth anniversary in March 1993. The issue was Mary Kaye's last; Christina was now Jane's number two and the day-to-day commander in chief. A natural writer, Christina was the easy choice for Mary Kaye's replacement, but she had never edited before and couldn't finesse the business side of the magazine the way Jane could. Whereas Jane had easily cozied up to advertisers, Christina was notoriously headstrong. "With Christina, if anyone like Dale Lang said, 'You shouldn't do that,' she would ignore it," says Mary. Lang agrees: "She's such a great person behind the scenes, but maybe it was too hard for her with advertising. I don't think she likes doing it. It's not her forte." Christina, for her part, admits, "I don't think they thought I presented so well, in my undershirts and jeans."

"I remember being a fly on wall in the art department when Karmen Lizzul [*Sassy*'s last art director] would present the cover and Christina worked out what should go on the cover," Amy Demas, the magazine's associate art director, remembers. Linda Cohen, the publisher, would come in and talk about cover lines—typical for someone in her position—and her input would

drive Christina crazy. "There was so much tension in the room it was unbelievable," Amy says. "And we sort of listened to what Linda had to say, but probably did our own thing anyway."

The business and editorial sides of *Sassy* had long been at odds. It was the business staff, after all, that had to deal with conservative advertisers, many of whom still wrongly thought of *Sassy* as a more risqué publication than *Seventeen* and *YM*. It didn't matter that *Sassy* had barely covered sex for years. "Everyone talked about this magazine that was risky with the sex articles, which is so irritating because we weren't even allowed to write about sex at all after the first issue, and it persisted for another six years," says Christina, characteristically hyperbolizing a bit. "It was written about in one article, and then it got passed on, but it's not true at all."

But because advertisers were nervous about *Sassy*'s image, there were still unwritten rules that they expected the magazine's editors to follow. After the boycott, Halfin had pledged to companies that the magazine would straighten up, reminding them that Lang's magazines had a history of squeaky-clean content. Still, Lang wasn't taking any chances, and appointed Halfin to approve the magazine's table of contents every month. Halfin was so intent on getting and keeping advertisers in the fold that she was happy to breach the usual church-and-state divide. "There was one article that was very graphic about a boy who went to rape counseling, and I wasn't sure if that was over the line or not, personally. So I basically sent the article to an advertiser just to get an opinion from her," says Halfin. "And her husband was a rape counselor, and he thought it was fine." That time the article ran, but more often than not the editorial side was held in check. "There were certain taboo things that we couldn't approach. I think it was abortion, homosexuality—the very things we wanted and needed to talk about. We would have to cut things or change things for the advertisers," Jessica says. "It was a creepy form of censorship because they weren't saying you *can't* do it, but rather 'If you do it, you won't get our money.' "

Of course, there were advertisers who understood *Sassy*. Calvin Klein and Guess Jeans were still fans, and the Coast Guard debuted an ad in *Sassy* depicting a female captain whose boyfriend brings her lunch. In fact, *Sassy* often had as many ad pages as did *YM*. But while most magazines were allowed to produce two or three editorial pages per advertisement, Lang didn't want to spend that kind of money, so *Sassy* could produce only one. "So if we had only thirty-five advertising pages, then we had seventy pages total," says Mary. "If people said, 'Well, why aren't we selling on the newsstand?' I'd say, 'Because it's a pamphlet!' Nobody's going to buy a pamphlet at a newsstand when they can buy this big *YM*, *Cosmo*, whatever." Newsstand numbers began to drop, and soon, fewer advertisers wanted in.

Sassy was undoubtedly the underdog when it came to circulation—*Seventeen*, *YM*, and *Teen* were all in the millions, while *Sassy*'s readership had stalled at 800,000 (a bigger audience, it should be noted, than those of many of the next generation of teen magazines). And yet it was

more expensive to advertise in *Sassy* than in its competition. In the early years, the magazine had justified the extra cost by touting *Sassy*'s high-quality paper stock, bigger size, and high-end photography and design. But after Cheryl and Neill decided to move on to new jobs elsewhere, *Sassy* underwent a series of unsuccessful redesigns. Art director Noël Claro did one in March 1992 that, while cute and zine-y, looked younger than previous incarnations. A 1993 redesign, though overseen by Cheryl, who returned briefly from Australia to work on the project, was boring and uninspired, from the smoothing out of the original paintbrush logo to the white backgrounds on almost all the covers. Mainstream stars like Jennie Garth and Tori Spelling, who were poked fun at in the pages of *Sassy*, suddenly graced its covers. The mandate was to keep the cover lines peppy and upbeat, make sure the model looks happy and approachable, keep the sex lines to a minimum (and small), and make sure the celebrities were plentiful; this was not the way to attract the kind of disaffected outsider girl who would create the next generation of *Sassy* readers. But the covers were battled over between the magazine's business and editorial departments. The end product was a diluted, compromised version of what each camp wanted, which made for a result that made no one happy.

Cohen thinks that the new look ultimately had a devastating effect on the magazine, with the unsophisticated design attracting a younger, less upscale, less coveted demographic: the average age of the *Sassy* reader, and the amount of discretionary income she made per week, dropped to below the levels of *Seventeen*'s readership. *Sassy* no longer stood out as a magazine for older teens, which had been key to its positioning.

In fact, the business concerns were endless. Most of the advertisers wanted to put their money into fashion- and beauty-focused publications, and *Sassy* had a reputation as being issue-oriented. Advertisers long had the mistaken idea that because *Sassy* readers thought of themselves as outside of the norm, they didn't want to buy the products other girls were buying; but if *Sassy* readers didn't want to buy Maybelline's frosty pink lipstick, they may have wanted to buy the red one. And even if they didn't want to buy pink plastic Caboodles makeup kits or Lane cedar chests, they were still avid consumers who wanted to buy Doc Martens and sailor tees to assert their identities. But the insider-y, hip, closed-off world *Sassy* increasingly represented made the magazine unappealing to big corporations. Cohen complained to Lang in a memo that companies thought that *Sassy* was "creating a subgroup of outcasts." She called the magazine "an elite club of alienated girls." Many of the magazine's readers would have agreed with her. So, in fact, would Jane: "When I went to the talk show, *Sassy* didn't have quite the clarity of vision. Mary Kaye was sort of a transitional person, and under Christina it definitely became edgier; circulation was lower, however, and the number of people who resubscribed was also lower. I definitely am more 'mass' than Christina is, and that's one reason the magazine did start to lose circulation."

In one undated memo, in a section titled "Offensive Collage," Cohen takes the editors to task:

Many articles seem to be inflected with anger, negativity, and offensive remarks. This is portrayed in such references as "Do you have a stick firmly lodged up your butt," and Christina's response to a reader letter, "Eat Me." Glossary definitions such as "Goob," meaning to cough up and spit out a ball of mucus from the back of one's throat or "Gadar, [sic]" which is the innate ability to tell at a glance if someone is gay, enabling "you to pinpoint whether an attractive morsel rides in your ranch or not" are inappropriate. One READ IT column reviews this book: "The Story of the Little Mole Who Went in Search of Whodunit," which is the story of a mole who emerges from his hole to find that another animal has "taken a dump" on his head and so goes in search of the culprit. This subject is unsuitable for a teenage mainstream magazine and offends our advertisers. The same is true for the as yet unmarketed device that allows a woman to stand up and pee. Language such as "This Sucks," "Bleed, Baby, Bleed," a reference to menstruation, and "You'd better thank me, bitches," is offensive. This anger is reflected back to us when we receive and print reader sentiments such as "When people say, 'I'm gonna kick your ass,' they don't kick your ass. They hit you in the face." Lynn and LaRue from Dugway, Utah, thought this magazine should be rated R. They said, "If you [print] a twelve-year-old's [letter] in your magazine, don't you think twelve-year-olds read it? We can tell by the way that you talk that you are a bunch of imbeciles." When it's turning off our audience, it's turning off our advertisers.

The *Sassy* editors hated Cohen. Margie remembers the staff putting their faith in one member of the ad staff who they thought understood them. "We were very hung up on this one ad salesman, Mike Fish." Fish worked primarily with record labels, but the lifeblood of any teen magazine is fashion and beauty advertisers. Fish's clients would not be enough to buoy the magazine, no matter how much the staff liked him.

Sassy was losing its buzz. Jane, preoccupied with her failing talk show and herself less a source of interest now that *Sassy* had reached its adolescence, wasn't bringing as much attention to the magazine as she used to. Cohen complained in a memo that "Our readers know all the editors—the public only knows Jane. We need to saturate the market with all the editors." The media world never caught on that there was more to *Sassy* than its editor in chief, and Lang wasn't willing to put more money into a PR and marketing budget to rectify the situation, which Mary

blames for the demise. "When it ended, it really had more to do with money—whether Lang had the money or didn't want to spend it on *Sassy*—and less to do with advertising," she says. "If the magazine had been owned by Condé Nast or Hearst and supported in a certain way, I think it would have been fine."

"There is a formula for consumer magazine success in America," says Professor David Abrahamson. "You have to come up with a very specific kind of editorial content that is of clear interest to a clear group of people to whom advertisers who tend to advertise in print want to sell products." *Sassy* solved the first two points—it had a clear voice and an audience that advertisers wanted to reach—but *Sassy* was not the vehicle advertisers wanted to use. Its singular voice was in many ways its downfall, and the decreasing ad pages and shrinking content wore on the staff in ways that only made matters worse.

"Writing, editing, and art direction is a job that's fun but requires a bit of passion. You could do other things and make more money. That's why it's a young person's sport," Abrahamson continues. "To do that under really contrary circumstances, from a defensive position, is really, really hard to do—there needs to be nurturing and protection to flourish. Once that shared enthusiasm on the part of editors gets severely dented, it's not too long before the product starts to show it. You can see magazines that are tired. There's no sort of binding energy, nothing animating."

In September 1993, *Sassy* hired Diane Paylor.

"As *Sassy*'s first African American writer, I knew I would be asked to write about issues of color. Who better to spew a little venom about racial prejudice than an everyday victim of it, huh?" Diane wrote in one story. *Sassy* had long been criticized for not being as racially sensitive as it could be. Kim regularly wrote about hip-hop, though it was never covered as much as the indie rock that Christina was partial to. Kim also wrote June 1991's "It's a Black Thing," about her experience as a white person interacting with the hostile members of Afrocentric black groups. The staff fought to get African-Americans, like Sassiest Girl in America Sala Patterson, on the cover. (The magazine industry has long believed that a black cover model is the death-knell to that month's circulation. But since publications didn't want to appear racist, they would put a black girl on the cover maybe once a year, usually in February, the shortest month and the one that got the smallest circulation numbers, anyway.)

Still, in *Sassy*'s pages, race never got as much play as did gender. For Diane's very first issue, the editors conjured up an article that was supposed to illuminate the disparity between blacks and whites. Diane and Mary Ann were both supposed to do regular day-to-day things like shopping at an expensive jewelry store and trying to get a cab at night. The goal was to see how differently Diane was treated because she's black. And a number of times racism was clearly an issue—Diane was falsely told that the store didn't sell men's jewelry, for example. But most of the time she was treated the same way that Mary Ann was.

And when she reported back to the *Sassy* staff, they told her to get back out there and try again, because not being treated badly wasn't a story.

"Finally she came into our office in tears and said, 'You don't understand what this is costing me. You don't understand what you're asking me to do, which is go and look for prejudice, which I live with every single day,' " says Kate Tentler, the magazine's final managing editor. "And we were like, 'Oh, fuck. Look what we're doing, we're just completely participating in this.' "

They told Diane to write about just that: about how her PC-spouting, injustice-fighting, liberal-minded editors were better at talking the talk than they were at being racially sensitive to the black people in their lives. Her resulting story, "With Friends Like These," chronicles the way an African American experiences ingrained prejudice at the hands of her supposed friends and colleagues. *Sassy* readers were mostly sympathetic. One wrote in to say, "Your story made me cry"; another said, "As an African-American reader, I understand exactly where you're coming from."

"I don't want to speak for Diane at all in this respect, but I did feel like it changed her feelings about being there," says Kate. "You live a lifetime of having to deal with this crap and then you think you're in a place where you're going to be safe and it clamps down on you again and it's just like, whoa. And particularly because *Sassy*'s MO was that it was an encouraging, accepting, inclusive place." (Diane was the only *Sassy* staff member who wouldn't speak on the record for this book.)

Editors and writers were fighting one another, and the only thing they were really bonded by was a shared venom toward their so-called leader. "It was like the magazine kept sinking, but things kept getting better and better for Jane," says Mike. Jane's fame continued to rise despite the fact that she had little involvement in the daily operations in the magazine that made her famous and her main project—the talk show—was a critical disappointment. Even the business staff was sick of the young, mediagenic editrix who had once brought them so much attention. "I have enjoyed working with Jane, but she hasn't been able to demonstrate a clear vision for this magazine," Cohen wrote in a memo to Lang.

If *Sassy* wasn't losing staff to burnout and boredom, they were losing them to larger publishers like Condé Nast. "I used to say to Si Newhouse [the company's chairman], 'I'm running a farm system for you over here. Every time we develop somebody into a talent you pick them off,' " says Lang. "And it wasn't just the money they were after. It was the great Condé Nast limousines, and all the perks." As the core staff began to turn over, finding new writers who could write in the *Sassy* voice without imitating any of its existing writers was difficult. "After *Sassy* had been out for a little while, people would come to work there—writers in particular—who had been reading *Sassy* and were trying to adopt the voice. That's never what I wanted. I just wanted them to write in their own, genuine voices. I can't tell you how many people would write in a style that was a parody of Christina Kelly, a not-as-good version of Christina Kelly," says Jane, who felt that

the original three staff writers (Christina, Karen, and Catherine) were the strongest they had. As Mike recalls, "Toward the end, there were pieces that were crap as far as I was concerned. I don't know how exactly it happened, but I think it was maybe the text itself wasn't as sparkling as it had been. And we were pretty beaten down by that point. I don't know if that's an excuse or a reason, but we just were." Said Cohen, in a memo, "What used to be a fun slumber-party conversation that made everyone feel welcome seemed more like a conversation that would take place in a smoky New York coffeehouse."

Of course, many readers who came of age during *Sassy*'s twilight years vehemently disagree. "Maureen Callahan made me want to keep reading and reading," says Max Weinberg. Liz Menoji's favorite staffer was Margie, who "wrote like I felt." Still, *Sassy*'s readers were growing up. *Sassy*'s initial teen audience was reaching college age and moving on to other magazines, or even to the sharp-tongued zines they had been introduced to in "What Now." "*Sassy* started to get old, and the *Jane Pratt* show really nailed the coffin shut. It was cooler to buy Franklin Bruno records about Jane than to listen to the *Sassy* house band, Chia Pet. Once the corporate shuffles started, I dropped my subscription and looked elsewhere for reading pleasure," says Marc Butler, a longtime *Sassy* fan who wrote for the first reader-produced issue. Jessica Nordell was sixteen in 1994 when she started drifting apart from *Sassy*. "I think I was kind of down on *Sassy*. I felt like it was trying too hard. I thought maybe there was

more to life than just wearing thrift-store clothing and tromping around. It was suddenly easier for me to make fun of it, whereas three years before I worshipped it."

countdown to the end

By early 1994, Jane hadn't been a part of daily life at the *Sassy* offices for a few years. "Jane was completely not around," says Christina. "I remember I was really not happy being the editor, and I went to her and said, 'I think I'm going to leave and be a freelance writer,' and she said, 'Yeah, I think you should.' I was expecting that she'd protest and tell me I had to stay, like she always had, whenever I'd gotten any kind of job offer. It was like she knew that something was being planned, that Dale was going to sell the magazine, so she was off trying to figure out what her next thing was." Amy remembers Christina and Jane's relationship as especially fraught during those last days. "Jane was not being super straightforward with her, and she'd been with Jane since the beginning. Christina was running the show every day and didn't feel Jane was being honest with her—she didn't feel she had the insider information. There was extreme tension between them. Everybody felt that. That was no secret."

Jane maintains that Lang didn't make her privy to any secrets, but she had begun to look elsewhere for a new project nonetheless. "I was hearing from women in their twenties who were saying, 'I'm twenty-six, I'm still reading *Sassy*. Come on, let's do something for women my age,

there's nothing! There's nothing for *Sassy* readers to graduate to.' I felt like I had done what I wanted to do with *Sassy*. I really wanted to start the next generation," she says. Lang Communications didn't have the money to develop a new magazine, so in spring of 1994, Jane left for Time, Inc., to start a magazine for twentysomething women. Still, Jane swears, "I would have much preferred to stay and still have some involvement with *Sassy*." Even though Jane had severed ties with *Sassy* and Lang Communications, it was business as usual in the pages of *Sassy*, with her signing "Diary" each month and still being credited as editor in chief.

Meanwhile, rumors of a sale were escalating and advertisers, thinking the magazine was unstable, were running scared. Lang sent a memo on September 27, 1994, to the *Sassy* staff: "It is with deep regret that I must inform you *Sassy* magazine is being put up for immediate sale . . . I want all of you to know I've done everything possible to avoid this action. *Sassy* is a potentially great magazine and you are a fine young group of professional magazine people. You both deserve a chance that I can no longer provide."

It was a long month. Christina immediately demanded an all-staff meeting, at which one of Dale's underlings made an unconvincing bid to assure his employees that they shouldn't worry about job security. Jane made a rare appearance in the office. But instead of calming the nerves of the staff she had, in one way or another, led for the last seven years, Jane announced the launch of her new magazine at Time, Inc.—six months

after she had gotten the job. "I think she even said, 'There's all these rumors that I'm going to do another magazine. And it's going to be called *Jane*,'" reports Mary. "It was kind of weird." Christina remembers Jane saying, "When I start it I'm going to hire you all."

In the meantime, though, the *Sassy* staff was stuck in a limbo of quasi-employment. Management began holding daily meetings to inform the beleaguered employees whether they should show up for work the next day. At one, Lang announced that he was looking for a bidder that would continue *Sassy*'s editorial mission and that his goal was to make a seamless transition. Then the staff was told not to complete work on the January 1995 issue, which was to be celebrity-produced (a format Jane would later use at *Jane*), with Liz Phair on the cover.

No one had anything to do, but the staff technically still had jobs, so they would while away their time with projects born of frustration. "We would all come in every morning to see if there was any news. Sort of mope around, put through invoices. I remember we were taking Polaroids," says Christina. They put the photos up on a big board in the office, chronicling the final days. The shots included "Christina signing Virginia O'Brien's expense report for the last time" and "Janet takes down the disco ball"; and, Christina remembers, "There were pictures of me holding up the sign WILL EDIT FOR FOOD." The bored staff also made a fake mock-up of the next issue. "It was filled with all these stories that we were obviously never going to be able to write, making fun

of specific advertisers, because we knew that the end was coming," Margie recalls. Instead of working, Mike would go see matinees of *Pulp Fiction*, and would sometimes stop by to see if anything was happening in the office. People sat in their cubicles and updated their résumés. He remembers, "I was under the delusion that we'd all have no problem getting jobs because the industry just loves *Sassy*. And, you know, we'd be snatched up in no time." (But it turned out that with the recession in full bloom, it wouldn't be so easy for them to land full-time employment.)

Then, for a brief, shining moment, it was rumored that Jann Wenner might be the staff's unlikely knight in shining armor. Wenner, the founder of *Rolling Stone* and the Wenner media empire, was known for being difficult. Still, he was admired as an editor who was eager to go against the grain—and, as an added bonus, he had cushy offices. On October 12, *Publishers Weekly* reported that Wenner had put in a bid for *Sassy*. The report turned out to be untrue.

On Friday, October 14, the daily staff debriefing at four p.m. ended with the news that on Monday would be their final meeting. That night, everyone went to a party that Karmen and Amy had been planning for a while, at a loft on the Bowery. Amy says, "It became the end-of-the-magazine party and it was a blast, a great night."

That Monday, October 17, after a morning spent shuffling between the conference room and their desks, nervously waiting for news, the staff was called together. Lang announced that *Sassy* had been sold. Christina remembers Halfin saying that Lang had spent his fortune on the magazine. "And I'm like, 'Whatever.' I'd been there for seven years, and I got one month's severance pay."

The buyer was Los Angeles–based Petersen, proud publisher of such trade publications as *Guns & Ammo*, *Hot Rod*, and a *Sassy* arch-nemesis, *Teen*. It was the only company to bid on *Sassy* that could come through with the money, which Dale needed to keep the rest of his titles afloat. "Petersen felt it was a good fit with *Teen* and gave them a larger share of the teen market between the two magazines," says Lang. *Teen* was largely read by girls between the ages of twelve and fifteen, and *Sassy* was supposed to appeal to older readers. "It was the wrong place, absolutely the wrong place for *Sassy* to go because it was totally run by bookkeepers. I'm sorry I ever had to sell it," Lang admits. Ira Garey, who had been a publisher of *Seventeen*, was brought in as joint publisher of *Sassy* and *Teen*. He recalls that *Sassy* was relatively inexpensive and that Petersen paid a little over a million dollars for it.

The night they found out that *Sassy* was sold, the staff went to the International Bar in the East Village. "I have a really good idea for the next issue," someone joked, or "That's such a good band for 'Cute Band Alert'!" Christina says they were just trying to make fun out of their bad luck. "We were just pretending that we were crazy people who didn't realize that we didn't have jobs anymore."

The next day, the unemployment office was the site of an impromptu *Sassy* staff reunion for Christina, Virginia O'Brien, Amy Demas, and Andrea Linnett. Jane, of course, wasn't there; she was busy with her new project. "I think that kind of soured people," says Mary. "I think they felt like, 'Well, we just lost our jobs, and Jane already has this great gig.' " The staff was shell-shocked. In fact, Christina had met with Petersen a few months prior when they were looking for an editor in chief at *Teen*. "And I think at that point they were considering buying *Sassy*, and I guess they were trying to assess what the situation was," she says. She told them she didn't think *Sassy* could be run from L.A. They thanked her for her time and dismissed her.

Back in the offices, the staff hadn't even been allowed to clean out their desks; everything belonged to Petersen now. Jennifer Baumgardner got the building's handyman to take her from the *Ms.* offices to the now-abandoned *Sassy* offices. "I walked in there, and all their files were still there, all their computers were still on. I mean, they were just told to leave," she says. Even the fruit chandelier, which had been immortalized in "Diary," was on the floor. "They just cut it down like they were cutting down a hanged person, and it just crashed onto the ground and was broken. And none of them ever came back to their offices," she says. "It was like Pompeii."

stepford *sassy*

After a curious three-month absence, loyal *Sassy* readers eagerly plucked the March 1995 issue from the newsstands. "I knew right away something had happened—the logo was in this horrible shade of neon, and the girl on the cover looked really corny and fresh-faced and false," says Julianne Shepherd. Someone else's signature was on "Diary," and "What Now" didn't have a single snarky reference, nor any hint of Christina's crankiness. In fact, there was no Christina. And no Mary, Margie, or Andrea. And who were Betsy and Caroline and Nina?

After anxiously wondering where the magazine had disappeared to, readers soon discovered that *Sassy* had undergone a complete change of staff and editorial philosophy, rendering it a kind of "Stepford *Sassy*," as *Bust* magazine called it. "It was as if a best friend, someone we used to go on pro-choice marches with, staying up late eating Mallomars and talking about vibrators, had turned up after a long trip with a bad case of amnesia—giving us blank looks when we started talking about 'restrictive gender roles' and blowing us off to go to the movies with her boyfriend," said *Bitch* magazine cofounder Lisa Jervis in "Kicking Sass," an article in *Salon*.

"The original vision for *Sassy*, there was really nothing wrong with," Jay Cole, *Sassy*'s executive publisher (who was also *Teen*'s publisher), told Daniel Radosh in a *New York Press* article at the time of the relaunch. "It was designed to give teens a sense of inner self-confidence, to develop self-respect, to empower young women. That concept is something we're planning to continue." Sound okay so far? "We're planning to use a lot of personalities, celebrities who have accomplished something, to give teens a sense of how they can be the best that they can be." And, he continues, "There will be a lot more fashion and beauty."

The new vision was incredibly misguided. Nothing about the new *Sassy* earned the trust of its old audience. Cole opined that "there were some issues of *Sassy* that were somewhat irresponsible. We have to be responsible not only to readers, but to parents and advertisers as well." He cites the "fringe-type" articles that were so beloved by readers. "There's no point in saying, 'the prom sucks,' " he says, sounding like he has zero knowledge of the teen-girl psyche.

So, in a sneaky ploy, the revamped *Sassy* tried to substitute the same breathless content so perfected by *Teen*—but flavored with the same outspoken style as the old *Sassy*. The language, which was affected and laughably "hip," was especially off. Compare the old *Sassy*'s "Mary asked me to go to Los Angeles for a beauty symposium. I thought, 'Bummer, there goes the weekend,' " with the new copy: "So you look mah-ve-lous in your high-school prom pic, but the then-love-of-your-life has since turned out to be a major creep-o-la. What's a gal to do?"

The Petersen-owned *Sassy* kept a few of the magazine's original columns, but they were the same in name only. "It Happened to Me" remained, but now included cheesy *YM*-style reenactments of the action contained within, like the shadowy portraits of a model looking on in disgust as her "mom" snorts a line in "My Mother Was a Coke Fiend." "What Now, What Next?" was supposed to be a revamp of the much beloved "What Now" column, but it lacked Christina's deadpan writing style and any sense of what was cool or important. "I was horrified to discover that concepts I invented were being defiled monthly by this clueless new staff," Christina wrote in *Ms.* Every month the column began with a "*Sassy* or Sissy" list, which was the new staff's way of conveying what was in and out. (*Sassy* and sissy are, in their warped version of the teenage universe, as follows: hackers and slackers; cuddlecore and riot grrl [sic]; thongs and bongs; skydiving and stagediving; Mattus nonfat ice cream and cellulite cream.) The new *Sassy* covered zines, but often missed the point that they were cut-and-paste affairs—one "Zine of the Month," *Foxy*, is a colorful endeavor produced by a big-name skate company.

Similarly, instead of pro-girl, unapologetically feminist articles, the new *Sassy* offered outdated and offensive advice about just about everything. On flirting: "Men think about sex all the time—some studies show as much as six times an hour. So any given time you're flirting with one of them, there's a chance he's wondering what you look like without your clothes on." Sounding like it was from a blame-the-victim, well-she-asked-for-it school of sexual assault, the magazine then went on to warn girls not to flirt with anyone inappropriate. In contrast to the original *Sassy*'s groundbreaking health stories, which put a primacy on female pleasure, there was now a sex column from two men: the conservative TV doctor Dr. Drew and former MTV *Headbanger's Ball* host Riki Rachtman. Sex education, in the Petersen *Sassy*, insisted that most "girls get emotionally attached after they've had sex with a guy. Guys usually do not." The empathy that *Sassy* had always

shown its teen subjects was decidedly absent. For instance, the article "(Un)planned Pregnancy: Teen Moms Tell All" calls one girl it profiles—a teenage mother of a baby who is again pregnant—"a living, breathing statistic."

And forget the original *Sassy*'s love-your-body-as-it-is ethic. "The prettiest things under the sun are super body-conscious (and, luckily, so are you)" read the copy of one fashion article, effectively shaming the reader into an image obsession or fueling the one she likely already had. Instead of "13 Reasons to Stop Dieting" there was "Safe Munching: Are You Sabotaging Your Diet?" In the place of Kim, Mike, and Margie sampling junk food, the new *Sassy* advised readers in "The Munchies: Defined and Defeated" to eat fruit when they craved candy, advocating the kind of calorie-counting lifestyle one would expect from *Seventeen*. The few times the new *Sassy* used the F-word—*feminism*—it was usually to discredit it, with the words *feminist PC thought police* appearing, in one article, in extra-large type. Another article that tackles women's rights, "Feminism 2000," states that "if it's hard for you to relate to the rules written by old-school feminists (you know, the ones who broke so much ground and burned so many bras back in your mom's day), you're not alone."

For former staff members, seeing *Sassy* reincarnated as the very teen drivel they despised was like a slap in the face. "I still have [the new version]," says Mary. "It is so awful." And "I remember the first issue," Jane says. "It had the calorie counts of your favorite fast foods on a page. And I actually started to cry there, at the newsstand, so I didn't finish reading it. I thought it was the most horrible, upsetting thing in the world. It was one thing to shut *Sassy* down. It was another to perpetuate the very thing that we had been fighting so hard against for eight years. I was like, 'Here we go, backwards.' "

Receiving the new, bad *Sassy* in the mail was also a defining moment for many fans. "I remember pulling that issue with Liv Tyler on the cover out of my mailbox and thinking, 'Uh-oh.' Then I opened it, and the new editor had her hair in a *ponytail*, with a sporty scrunchie. I cancelled my subscription that very day," says Laura Padilla. Alice Tiara spent an evening with a friend, systematically ripping the issue to shreds. Disposing of the new *Sassy* was a way for fans, in a small way, to voice their dissent. "All I remember is that I got the Petersen *Sassy* and hated it so much that I threw it in the fireplace," says Maria Tessa Sciarrino.

Elisa Ung, a *Sassy* fan who was in high school at the time of the change, remembers her first glimpse of the new issue and realizing that everything she had loved about her favorite magazine was gone. "It was such a shock to my fragile teenage system. It was like someone had died. It was like all of my crew had jumped ship." She emailed *Sassy*'s old address in a desperate attempt to reach someone on the New York staff, saying that even though the old *Sassy* was gone, she would always be grateful because it taught her to have her own voice. "Margie wrote back and said thanks and that my email was wonderful. Her response was seriously a highlight of my teenage

years." Kate Tentler was using her period of unemployment to lie on the couch and watch the O. J. Simpson trial, when she got a call from a thirteen-year-old reader from Vermont, who had found her number through information. She wanted to know what the staff was up to, and had one more question: Why don't they just start their own magazine? Readers, reared on zines and blissfully ignorant of the costs of mainstream publishing, wondered why the staff had let the powers-that-be at Petersen get them down.

"I remember feeling really cheated, like it was way too soon for it to go. I was like, 'No! I still need you!' " remembers Michael Kilmis. Sarah Lynn Knowles saw *Sassy*'s revamp as an indication of the generational divide: "It proved how little adults understood teen girls. I never felt a wider, more infinite gap between teens and adults. I remember feeling shocked, rendered speechless." For fans of *Sassy* who were beginning to age beyond their teen years, *Sassy*'s demise was a metaphor for the compromised world of adulthood. "The sale happened my first year of law school," says Rita Hao. "I was miserable and doing finals and kept wondering where my *Sassy* was. I was waiting for my grades to come back, and I got this crappy *Sassy* and it made me feel like all good things eventually sell out. I'm a sellout, too! I was totally depressed. I thought, 'This is what happens to me for going to law school.' I was in a bad mood for the rest of the summer." She later started a Web page devoted to eulogizing the old *Sassy* and tracking the whereabouts of former staffers. Ocean Capewell felt similarly "adrift in the world" after *Sassy* was gone. "I re-member writing a list of the bad things that had happened to me that year, and the death of *Sassy* was at the top," she says. "I literally mourned the folding of that magazine and was depressed about it for months, as if it were a living, breathing thing that had died."

Scores of readers voiced their dissent about the new content, writing angst-filled letters to the new publication. Sarah Kowalski was a sophomore in high school when the new *Sassy* appeared. Her let-ter, which she has now published on her blog, fea-tures such laments as "I am saddened and angered that such a beautiful, intelligent, and worthwhile in-stitution has been corrupted. Everything I enjoyed and admired in the old magazine is dead." Many other readers agreed with her about the new content, but predating the widespread technology of online bulletin boards by a few years, it was difficult for them to commiserate with fellow distraught teens.

In the January 1996 issue (which also fea-tured an interview with Wilson Phillips singer Chynna Phillips on the joys of being young and married), the Petersen editors made the rather bizarre decision to publish fourteen letters on the magazine's letter page—unaptly titled "Pushing the Envelope"—from livid *Sassy* fans. They titled the collection "Best of the Hate Mail."

"The only reason I even look at the new *Sassy* is so I can phone my friends and trash it. My friend has burned her *Sassy*s," Samantha Conover wrote, adding that she suggests they "beg Jane, Diane, Margie, and all the old staff to come back, and maybe I'll forgive you."

Other fans also weighed in. Jenna Harrison wrote, "You have sucked every ounce of what the 'old' *Sassy* stood for out of the magazine. This magazine contains nothing but superficial garbage that needs to be thrown away forever. How could you do this to us? We depended on *Sassy* month to month for advice, security, and most of all, a good friend. You're like a guy who broke up with us without a real reason." Others lament the loss of the old staff members with the kind of vitriol only a scorned teen could muster up: Kyla Brown says, "I miss Jane. What did you do with her? I pray every night that a huge earthquake hits Cali-fornia; maybe then I can have my old *Sassy* back!"

But even more bizarre than publishing hate mail that name-checked the old staff was the mag-azine's response to its new readers, under the headline "*Sassy* Suggests: Get over It! Get a Clue! Get a Life!" It read:

Jane's gone. She checked out way before Petersen Publishing bought *Sassy* (to save its individual voice within the youth mar-ket from extinction—you can only offend our readers, their parents, and your adver-tisers so many times before they call it quits) to pursue talk-show stardom and other flights of celebrity fancy (and we're star-idolizing?).

As to many of the other old *Sassy* staffers, they are currently contributing to such groundbreaking, forward-thinking and *mainstream* magazines as *Rolling Stone, Entertainment Weekly*, and *Elle*. While we respect their work, we're not them, don't want to be them, don't want to adopt their writing style, and refuse to insult your intelligence by trying to sound like them. We're us . . . and unlike the former staffers, or Madonna, Elvira, Iman, and Cher, we're kind of attached to our last names!

As to the writers of the above-printed paeans to pissiness: First, we'd like to say that we've gotten tons of positive, encouraging mail—and **our** share of letters that made some wonderful suggestions on how we could improve our magazine. We appreciate that so much! But as to the nasty letters, when we first started receiving those missives, we found them amusing. But then we began to feel bad . . . a little for ourselves but also for you! That you are capable of such whiny evil is disheartening and pretentious. Quit your bitchin', lighten up, and cut us some slack. We welcome all criticism so long as it's constructive, but very few of the hate letters are the least bit enlightening or illuminating.

We're not saying we're perfect, but one thing we do know is that *Sassy* caters to eclectic tastes, not some exclusive girls [sic] club for the terminally hip. What we relate to are readers whose minds are not just bright but open; who have a sense of humor as well as a sense of style; and who aren't too cool to have fun.

To those girls who get it, the real fun-

smartgroovygoofygreat girls, we say: Welcome to *Sassy* '96 . . . and beyond!

To this day, none of the former Stepford *Sassy* staffers have commented on what they hoped to accomplish with such a mean-spirited, bitter, and vindictive letter to their readers.

Jane remembers reading her name in the despised new *Sassy*, accusing her of checking out, and likens it to "a mother saying, 'Your father just ran off, he doesn't want you!' It was like, 'Oh my god, my poor readers!' "

But nothing could be done to bring *Sassy* back from the grave. After all, Lang didn't sell *Sassy* because of unpopularity or lack of loyalty from its readership. For some, the very presence of the new *Sassy* served as a nagging reminder that the glory days were over. Fan Cheryl Taruc illustrates this, saying that the mere act of catching a glimpse of the new *Sassy* would leave her "feeling ashamed when I saw it on the newsstand. I couldn't even look at it."

Predictably, the revamped *Sassy* failed. In 1996 Petersen folded *Sassy* into now-defunct *Teen*. Petersen couldn't afford to maintain two separate teen publications with virtually the same content and identity. So *Sassy*, whose history was much less advertiser-friendly, was out. The new *Sassy*'s failure was seen by former staffers and fans as a kind of victory. The ultimate irony was that *Teen*, in many ways *Sassy*'s nemesis, prevailed (though not for long; the monthly edition of the print magazine soon folded).

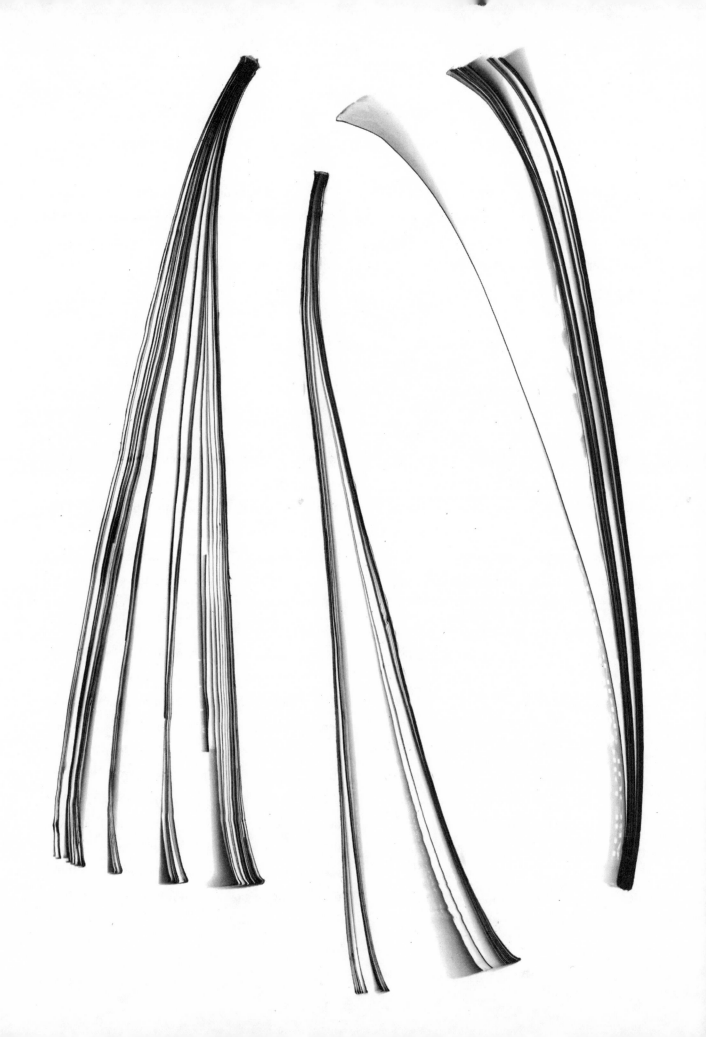

chapter 8

instant nostalgia

If magazines best represent the time in which they were created, then *Sassy* is the ultimate avatar of its era. "*Sassy* was to 1991 what *Playboy* was to its moment," says Ann Powers. *Playboy* helped create an ideal of martini-swilling, urban men-about-town for the average American guy; *Sassy* created an equally potent image for young women. Powers surmises that *Sassy* created a "fantasy of liberation for different people. One fantasy was for fifteen-year-old girls, and another was for twenty-eight-year-

old men. I don't think anything now holds that space."

That's why, years later, so many readers can't stop talking about *Sassy*. "It's kind of funny how cultlike *Sassy* fans can be," says Ocean Capewell. "I remember when I was eighteen, standing in the kitchen of my first apartment with one of my roommates as she chopped Vidalia onions. She asked if I'd ever had them before. I said no, but I remembered that the girl in the sorority article in *Sassy* said she was from Vidalia, Georgia, and it was the sweet-onion capital of the world. My roommate looked at me in shock and said, 'That's what our other roommate said! That exact sentence!' " And back issues of *Sassy* hold up surprisingly well—not just for fans to reread, but for a new generation of teens. Capewell's teenage sister, who was five when *Sassy* folded, found her copies and has, as Capewell puts it, "become obsessed. Even though she doesn't really get the pop-culture references, she's really in love with its utter sassiness. I think it's really exciting that the message can still get out there. I mean, who cherishes copies of *Seventeen* from ten years ago?"

Former staffer Karen Catchpole spent four years backpacking through South Asia in the post-*Sassy* years. "I remember being in Burma, and we must have been doing introductions and talking about what we do at home. And then the lightbulb went off in this woman's head and she said, 'What's your last name?' She went bananas—*bananas*—to the point where I was like, 'Lady, this is kind of getting embarrassing.' She was like, 'You saved my life. I loved the magazine. Oh, what happened? And who killed it? And I'm really mad.' "

"It's still my favorite thing, when someone comes out of the woodwork and talks about *Sassy*," says Kim France, who was speaking at her alma mater, Oberlin, years after *Sassy* folded. She mentioned having worked at *Sassy* and said, " 'I don't know how many of you guys remember or read it?' And all these hands went up."

There are also myriad heartbreaking stories of how *Sassy* collections lovingly amassed during the teen years were lost. Alice Tiara started crying when she found out her mother had accidentally thrown away her collection—"I was absolutely dumbfounded that she didn't realize how much *Sassy* had meant to me"—but salvation came when her best friend showed up with a duffel bag full of *Sassys* she had gotten from Craigslist. Now Alice has five years' worth of back issues organized in chronological order in her bedroom and reads them "whenever I'm feeling nostalgic for some hot nineties clothing or feminist zeal."

Some fans wanted to give the magazine a permanent place online. *Blair*, created by Richard Wang and Bryan Nunez, is a Webzine so *Sassy*-esque that it even had a "Cute Skater Alert." It was once described as being "like *Tiger Beat* for a smarter person, but not *that* much smarter." Their first issue, in winter 1994, eulogized the old *Sassy*. Wang had long had an email relationship with Margie, which turned into a relationship with many staff members; he went to Andrea's thirtieth birthday party and watched Christina dance to "Superfreak"—the highlight of his night. He and Mary even bonded over whether Clark Wallabees and Ugg boots were ripe for a comeback, and she later leaked the *Sassy* celebrity issue to him. The lost issue of *Sassy* was renamed *Sissy*, not just as a tribute to the teen magazine's gay fans but also so Wang and Nunez would not get sued. In it, Chloë Sevigny posed as Edie Sedgwick, Joey Ramone went to a spa, Mayim Bialik wrote a guide on how to perform a mitzvah, and drag queen RuPaul guest edited

"Zits and Stuff." "Now what magazine could bring all those people together?" Wang asks.

In November 1996, Jennifer Baumgardner hired Christina to write about the last days of *Sassy* for *Ms.* "I was finally getting a sense of how important *Sassy* was to feminism," she says. The article almost didn't happen: Jennifer remembers Marcia Gillespie, *Ms.*'s editor in chief, reading Christina's article and declaring, "We're not running it. *Sassy*'s not important. Christina just sounds whiny." Indeed, Christina's trademark exasperation is evident: "Now, this insult to the memory of *Sassy*-as-we-intended-it-to-be is dead and gone. And I'm supposed to feel . . . what? Vindicated? Happy? Relieved? To tell you the truth, I don't feel much of anything." Jennifer was given the order to find another writer and another topic, but she refused. "It was much better than a lot of the shit we ran—a lot more sparkling and new and feminist. A lot of the stuff we ran felt like, 'Well, people should probably know this by now because they've been reading *Ms.* for the last twenty-five years.' It felt different," she says. Gillespie finally caved. Christina's essay ran and received bagfuls of letters from *Ms.*'s younger readers, who were thrilled that Christina and *Sassy* were being name-checked in the premier feminist publication. Paying lip service to *Sassy*'s death made the older Second Wave feminists at *Ms.* at least appear to understand the younger generation of Third Wavers, which was a bridge they needed to build if they were going to stay vital as these new feminists came of age.

mega zines

"It was like what they say about the Velvet Underground—everyone who listened to them started a band. Everyone who read *Sassy* started a zine," says Rita Hao. *Sassy*'s zine boosterism primed its readers for indie media. When the magazine folded, many longtime *Sassy* fans, frustrated both by how their favorite magazine was treated by mainstream publishing and by the lack of *Sassy*-like alternatives, delved deeper into the world of alternative publications. Across the country, zines were started as a grassroots response to *Sassy*'s demise, and some grew to be nationally circulated publications.

In 1993, Marcelle Karp and Debbie Stoller met as twentysomethings when both were working creative corporate jobs at Nickelodeon. They bonded over being devoted *Sassy* readers, outside of the target teen demographic, and wished that something with a similar sensibility existed for women their age. In their off-hours they began hoarding the company's office supplies so they could start a paper-and-staple zine called *Bust*. It had an open, inviting, exploratory approach to sex; was obsessed with Hello Kitty; and celebrated 1950s pinup Bettie Page. There were fun, feminist-y columns like "One Handed Read" (short erotica pieces); an entire issue devoted to gay men; and "News from a Broad," global news coverage of women's issues. "The style and the language of *Bust* came really directly from what the girls were doing at *Sassy*," says Karp. In fact,

Stoller and Karp became friends with Christina ("I met her because we were at a party and we were both crushing, I think, on the same guy," says Karp). *Bust* even flirted with mainstream circulation when the Internet media company Razorfish bought it in 2000. Unlike the staff at *Sassy*, Stoller and founding creative director Laurie Henzel were able to buy back the magazine after the dot-com bubble burst and make it into a smaller-scale success.

Similarly, Chicago-based *Venus* magazine was started by avowed *Sassy* fan Amy Schroeder. "Growing up, my family moved around quite a bit and I was shy, so *Sassy* made me feel like, 'Hey, it's okay to be different and to challenge the norm,'" she says. "*Sassy* inspired me to daydream about one day working for a magazine and living in New York. If it weren't for *Sassy*, I'm not sure if I would have entered the publishing world." She started *Venus Zine* while she was still in college as a venue to write about girls in music, film, and print, and it read a bit like a magazine-sized "Cute Band Alert." After a brief stint working in publishing in New York postgraduation, she started stepping up *Venus*'s publishing schedule and ultimately made it her full-time job.

Andi Zeisler and Lisa Jervis grew up together in New York City, and each of them interned at *Sassy*. In 1995, after graduating from Colorado College and Oberlin—two of the Sassiest Colleges in America—and shortly after *Sassy*'s death, they moved to San Francisco. The connoisseurs of high and low culture spent a lot of time reading zines and staring at the television, though they weren't always happy with what they saw. "It wasn't really that productive to be complaining to each other or shouting at the TV," says Zeisler. "There was something to be said from a feminist perspective, but we were stuck because, though we had a lot of ideas, as twenty-two-year-old retail workers we didn't have a lot of places to publish them." *Bitch: Feminist Response to Pop Culture*, began as a black-and-white zine printed at Kinko's with a circulation of two hundred, which would later grow to more than fifty thousand. Zeisler says that her adolescent devotion to *Sassy* was a big inspiration. "They were really foregrounding the lives of girls, and not in relation to boys or in relation to their parents. That's what we wanted to do with *Bitch*, in creating a feminist magazine that we would want to read." Jervis says that, for her, *Sassy* was responsible for "my love of magazines and magazine conventions, the way they're put together." Some memorable *Bitch* pieces include a love letter to *Buffy the Vampire Slayer*, a story on the rise of the word *lady*, and an investigation into the waxing and waning of men's body hair.

sassy diaspora

Bitch was one of the most vocal detractors of *Jane* magazine, the publication that should have been the most obvious heir to the *Sassy* throne. In 1997, Jane finally got the publication she had begun to work on in 1993 off the ground—not with Time, Inc., but with Fairchild, which owned

Women's Wear Daily and W. Sassy fans could rejoice—Jane brought Christina on as the launch executive editor; Karen later held the same position.

Lisa Jervis was initially thrilled at the news of a new magazine from Jane. "I thought it was going to be like Sassy, but for my age now. What a great antidote to that other crap," she says, referring to the other women's magazines out there. After reading the first two issues and feeling disappointed, Jervis penned a scathing review for Salon. She writes, "Those of us salivating in front of the newsstand were hoping for something that took Sassy's early vision of self-confident girl power and critical thinking a step further. I don't know why we thought that we could expect something different, something intelligent and even mildly subversive, something really good, from a corporate publisher." Like other Sassy readers, reared on a fantasy of liberation and DIY, Jervis was angry at being let down by Jane.

Jane and Christina were none too pleased with Jervis, whom they had specifically asked to send in story ideas for Jane's first issue (though none of them ended up in the magazine). The morning the Salon story ran, Jervis awoke to a seven a.m. phone call from Christina. "She called to yell and to suggest that I was bitter because they said no to the pitches. I was livid. I said I had read both issues cover to cover and wrote my honest opinion about them," says Jervis.

Thus began a long-running feud between the two publications. The editors at Bitch retaliated by compiling an article called "10 Things I Hate About Jane," which later spun off into a regular column called the "Jane Petty Criticism Corner," in which the editors devoted a thousand words per issue to the failings of the glossy twentysomething magazine. Jane's editors soon fired back a blind item about the anger of a certain feminist editor who they claimed really wanted to write for the magazine and had been shot down.

So why has Jane inspired so much fervor among Sassy devotees? According to Bitch: "Sad as it is, we're used to women's magazines making us feel that we're not thin or pretty enough or rich or well-heeled enough, and that's why many of us choose not to read them. But it's far worse to be smugly informed that what we're getting from Jane is different, when in fact the only difference lies in the pitch itself. Jane's snooty, preening reality is that much more painful for having the initial premise—and Pratt's own promises—dangled before us." Says Jessica Nordell, "I think the spirit of Sassy was one of creating stuff, and the spirit of Jane is consuming stuff. I always finished reading Sassy feeling good, and finished reading Jane feeling bad." Lara Zeises remembers being excited when Jane came out, but quickly feeling let down. "It was just Cosmo in a different dress. I read Jane and I think, 'Oh, God. Still working that smug superiority thing, aren't you?' "

A lot of the ire is directed at Jane herself, who left the magazine in August 2005. She's become the Liz Phair of the publishing world, and openly embracing fame and money has made her anathema to many former fans, as has her lighter take on feminism.

The promise that Jane was going to arrive

just as the *Sassy* generation was coming into adulthood was seductive, as if another Jane Pratt–helmed magazine, with Christina writing a "What Now" type of column called "Dish," could help girls navigate their grown-up lives. But maybe that's too much to expect from a magazine—even a purportedly feminist one. Jennifer Baumgardner says she experienced the same feeling even at *Ms.* "These things that are special things for women raise your expectations so much, and then you go in there and it doesn't provide a brand-new you, and it doesn't meet all of your creative needs, and you do get shot down and you do have to make compromises," she says. But compromise is exactly what a woman's magazine needs to do in order to survive—as any *Sassy* staff member can attest.

Surprisingly, Kim and Andrea have been looked upon more kindly by *Sassy* readers, who love *Lucky*, the popular Condé Nast magazine of which they are editor in chief and creative director, respectively. Though it's often dismissed as a glorified catalog, *Lucky* always takes a positive approach to the female figure—never disparaging or making fun—and a joyful, girlfriend-y approach to shopping. There is a pleasant lack of socialites in its pages, and an absence of *Absolutely Fabulous*–style fashionspeak. The magazine is playful, not didactic, and shows a wide range of price points. Plus, there's the added bonus of the edgy-but-wearable, classic approach to fashion that Andrea is known for. Kim says she was worried about the reaction to *Lucky* among former *Sassy* readers. "Sort of like, 'Kim France is a sellout,' "

she says. But not everyone agrees. "I think *Lucky* is really what became of *Sassy*," says former intern and X-girl co-creator Daisy Von Furth. "It's more of a real heir than *Jane*. Its obsession with detail—a lot of that was in *Sassy*." Even *Bitch* did a feature on their love for *Lucky*.

Other *Sassy* staffers have spread the *Sassy* aesthetic in both obvious and subtle ways in their prominent positions at publications including *YM* and *ELLEGirl* (Christina was editor in chief of both), *Entertainment Weekly* (where Mike Flaherty, Ethan Smith, and Mary Kaye Schilling have all worked), *Shop, Etc.* (Karen Catchpole), *Spin* (Charles Aaron, Maureen Callahan), and *Modern Bride* (Mary Clarke).

teen magazines

"The intriguing thing about *Sassy* is that it managed to make you feel really subversive and underground and rebellious and smart for basically doing what every other teenage girl was doing: reading teen magazines," says Melody Warnick, a *Sassy* reader.

Sassy left its mark on every teen magazine that followed it. During Christina's tenure, *YM* banned articles on dieting; covered such *Sassy*-esque stories as punk-rock Mormon teens; and featured models with braces. The now-defunct *ELLEGirl* mirrored *Sassy* perhaps most obviously—it was targeted to the alternative girl, now a bona fide persona. All teen magazines can thank *Sassy* for providing them with a new way to cover celebrities, mixing mainstream and indie culture. (Rita Hao sees this as something *Sassy* contributed to pop culture at large, "like how MTV plays Modest Mouse and then plays Hilary Duff—but that was totally unusual for its time.")

Sassy was the first teen magazine to acknowledge that not all teen girls have the same banal desires, and so was born the niche magazine for teens. Today's teen magazines recognize the need to cater to a psychographic, much like *Sassy* did fifteen years ago. Celebrity-obsessed girls could buy the now-defunct *Teen People*, or fashion addicts can pick up a copy of *Teen Vogue*. Atoosa Rubenstein, a former *Sassy* intern, was the founding editor of *CosmoGIRL!* "I loved *Sassy*, but I didn't love *Sassy* for the same reason that many people loved *Sassy*. I didn't necessarily relate to the girl they were speaking to," she says. "That girl was way edgier and cooler than I was. But what I really liked about it was that that girl was different. And I was different." *CosmoGIRL!* came complete with a trademark "you go girl" tone and a "Born to Lead" tagline. It was geared toward the geeky, overachieving crowd, and Atoosa offered herself up as a role model to teens who didn't fit in. "It was essentially a love letter to the girl I was, which was a misfit and sort of an outcast but not necessarily the cool outcast; in a way, *Sassy* made that girl cool. What about the other girl who's just truly dorky?" says Rubenstein, who was editor in chief of *Seventeen* from 2003 to 2006.

Of course, today's teen magazines aren't entirely like *Sassy*. (In fact, Tae Won Yu, a *Sassy* fan and former designer at *ELLEGirl*, describes the experience of working there as "an exercise in pandering to the lowest common denominator and promoting some sick, alienated vision of teenagers as lame jerks.") They are mostly adulatory toward celebrities, and they're more advertiser-friendly than ever before, especially now that luxury brands, like Dior, jeweler David Yurman, and Marc Jacobs, once relegated to women's magazines, are now targeting teen girls, and electronics companies—once the domain of teen boys—are shilling iPods, laptops, and video-game consoles. While teen magazines still show skinny models, feminism exists in the form of a love-your-body approach to clothes, more explicit sex education, and a general feeling of girl power—though none of these magazines would ever use the word *feminist* on their covers.

the media conundrum

Christina says she always wants to tell people "I'm so sorry to have gotten you into this career. Working at *Sassy* was totally different than working at any of the other magazines." Perhaps *Sassy*'s ultimate seduction was to sell the lives of its young, urban editors as the greatest version of adulthood imaginable. But the magazine world completely transformed in the years following *Sassy*'s demise. All the problems *Sassy* had in grappling with the mainstream media are still very much alive—if not more so. One of the effects of the recession of the 1990s was a publishing industry much less likely to launch new magazines. The climate of media conglomeration has resulted in big media companies that are un-likely to support overtly political publications, and magazines are more beholden to advertisers than ever if they want to stay afloat.

In some ways, independent magazines like *Bitch*, *Bust*, and *Venus Zine* feel utopian. With no large advertisers to contend with (their pri-mary advertisers are girl-friendly—and often girl-owned—companies that hawk vibrators, knitting patterns, and books), they have the absolute free-dom to say what they want. Schroeder, who is in-spired by *Sassy*'s wide circulation, is also cautious about the attached strings. "Some people think *Venus* could be like *Sassy*, but I don't know. It's harder and harder for magazines to jump in and do something different and still be big. I think about that a lot in my work now—and how it failed for *Sassy*, and how much that sucked."

Independent media has its share of problems as well. Just as *Sassy* could sometimes feel like it was setting up a rigid worldview to which readers had to subscribe, today's indie magazines can have an equally unwavering set of principles to adhere to, as if you must have a working knowl-edge of Hélène Cixous, help unionize the Lusty Lady strip club, and own the complete Sleater-Kinney oeuvre in order to be part of their clique. They've created their own vernacular, but it's a largely insular one. With small circulations, they're mostly writing for an audience that al-ready agrees with what they're saying, and what's more, a reader must have a certain access just to purchase the magazines, which aren't always available at big booksellers or at Wal-Mart. Ulti-mately, their greatest asset and their greatest downfall is that they aren't representative of the outside world.

In this diverse new media world, everyone wants to know: Could *Sassy* exist today? There are so many variables involved—political climate, economics—that it's impossible to say. But an even more interesting question might be: Would teenagers feel that they need it? In an increasingly wired world, girls look to one another for guid-ance. With popular social-networking Web sites like MySpace and Facebook, girls can connect to one another effortlessly, but the sites are devoid of any adult oversight, and therefore lack a certain authority. There is no one with more experience passing down advice—no Kim talking about what it's like to have an alcoholic parent, no Margie talking about life with a gay brother, no Mike telling you why the Ramones are so seminal, no Mary advising you to zap zits with toothpaste.

In fact, as magazines' importance in Ameri-can culture declines, it's another form of media that seems to have inherited most of *Sassy*'s quali-ties: blogs. They are often written in a first-person, transparent, stream-of-consciousness style that is very similar to the tone of *Sassy*. Countless former *Sassy* readers have their own blogs in which to ob-sessively chronicle a mix of pop culture, activism, and their personal lives. And the obsessive way that *Sassy* chronicled celebrities is readily apparent in blogs like Defamer, which covers stars' foibles, as does its sister site Gawker, which also dissects the incestuous Manhattan media scene. Blogs insist on the importance of their creators' voices; they assume that the writer has something worth saying, even (or especially) if it's just chronicling the seeming minutiae of their lives—a very feminist way of thinking of which *Sassy* was a proponent. And they are accessible and democratic in a way that zines never were, since more people have access to computers than to the independent bookstores and cafés that stocked the cut-and-paste creations of yore.

pop vs. politics

What made *Sassy* so special was that it created a persona for a teenage girl or adult woman who was both hip and engaged (a template that was taken up, somewhat readily, by indie rockers, gay men, and some straight men as well). The publication merged pop culture and politics, making a magazine seem like a viable realm to work out larger social questions.

"Though it likes a revolutionary pose, hip is ill-equipped to organize for a cause," notes John Leland in *Hip: The History*. In its heyday, *Sassy* was often accused of being socially aware without being truly socially active; even the magazine's last publisher, Linda Cohen, pointed this out in her marketing plan, which called on the magazine to get involved in social programs rather than just paying lip service to being politically engaged.

But maybe the distinction between pop culture and political engagement isn't entirely

useful. What *Sassy* did, as a mainstream magazine for teenage girls, was reimagine what it meant to be an American girl, and what it would mean to be an American adult woman. So what if 1992's "Year of the Woman" was a PR construct, a political sham, with only five women elected to the Senate? What *Sassy* did was to elevate girls, to put them at the forefront, to make them part of the cultural zeitgeist. To make them cool.

The years immediately following *Sassy*'s death saw an explosion of popular culture made for and marketed to girls—but it soon lost the hard edges of underground culture. Angry yet acceptable female musicians—sexy, styled, apolitical—abounded as Lilith Fair–style girl rockers such as Sarah McLachlan, Fiona Apple, and Alanis Morissette topped the charts. In 1997, Meredith Brooks was nominated for a Grammy for her one-hit wonder "Bitch," which posited female anger as one of many feminine postures, one that could attract a man—a riff on the old Madonna-whore duality. The riot grrrl movement's "revolution girl style now" message was depoliticized and diluted in the post-*Sassy* years, becoming the Spice Girls' vapid proclamation of "girl power!" "It's probably a fair assumption to say that 'zigazag-ha' is not Spice shorthand for 'subvert the dominant paradigm,' " observed Jennifer Pozner in a 1998 article about the Spice Girls in the magazine *Sojourner*. The idea of girl power didn't exist before *Sassy*; but post-*Sassy*, the girl-centric worldview the magazine espoused was watered down, turned into an appealingly sexy slogan silk-screened on a tight baby tee. Being a rebellious girl no longer necessarily involved marching for choice or taking back the night; all you had to do was show your thong.

Like all magazines, *Sassy* was wholly a product of its time. Not only was underground culture making its way into the mainstream, but a Democrat was elected to the White House, Third Wave feminism was galvanizing a new generation, and campus activism was at an all-time high. Since then, the political climate in the United States has certainly moved farther to the right. Fundamentalist groups like Focus on the Family, which seemed like a reactionary fringe group during its campaign against *Sassy*, have gained a larger following.

But the ways in which the world has changed only amplify why fans' nostalgia for *Sassy* runs deeper than just simple wistfulness for the grunge era. *Sassy* nostalgia is about revisiting the fantasy of a liberated adult life that the magazine promised its teen readers, a life that seems harder to live as the inevitable compromises of adulthood become imminent. It's not about longing for high school as the good old days before we got wrinkles or were saddled with grad-school debt or hadn't yet walked down the aisle. It's about longing for those moments that crystallized the *Sassy* ethic of engaged self-determination: the first time you read *Factsheet 5*, talked back to the TV, ordered a seven-inch from Simple Machines, stayed up late with your friends talking about sex, picked up a guitar, or marched for choice. It's about longing for a time when you really believed that you would be able to live *Sassy*'s ethos. To readers, *Sassy* is still about hope.

acknowledgments

. . . . .

How many people's lives did *Sassy* change? A lot. And many of them wrote or called or met with us to give us the details. Thanks to all the fans who shared their stories. Even if we didn't quote you directly, your thoughts had a huge influence on this book.

We appreciate the generosity of everyone we interviewed, so many of whom were willing to take a funny/poignant/interesting walk down memory lane with us. Our inner fifteen-year-olds are especially grateful to the *Sassy* staff; we certainly couldn't have done this without them. A very special thank you to Mary Clarke, the very definition of a connector, who helped set the wheels in motion.

Like most books, this one took two-plus years from conception to completion. We'd like to thank all our friends and colleagues who patiently spent that time asking, over and over, "So how is the book coming?" and pretending to be enthused about the answer. Special gratitude goes to Elspeth, proprietor of Podunk, the best tea shop ever, where we spent hours nibbling scones and getting all our best work done. The average boyfriend would be less than supportive if his girlfriend came home after a few drinks and announced that she was going to write a book with someone she had just met. Not Mike DeMaio. Kara would like to say: I love you and thank you for the endless counsel and support. And we'd both like to thank our parents. If it weren't for you, we may have grown up in more interesting hometowns and not needed *Sassy* to change our lives. Finally, all that adolescent angst has been put to good use.

Acknowledgments

Thank you to our agent, Sarah Lazin, a font of great advice; we look forward to a long relationship. And to Denise Oswald at Farrar, Straus and Giroux, who we secretly hoped would be our editor from the very beginning. She certainly did not disappoint. And we can't forget Paula Balzer; once we convinced her we had a book, she set about convincing everyone else.

We'd also like to express gratitude to our tireless interns, all of whom are an asset to the publishing industry: Rebecca Willa Davis, Maressa Brown, Vanessa Weber, Melanie Klesse, and Amy Bleier Long. Thanks to Sarah Almond, Sara Jane Stoner, and Jessica Ferri for patiently fielding so many random queries and to Liz Menoji for sending us every *Sassy* fan's dream care package.

index